C. Lynn Fox, Ph.D.

Other Books and Curriculum Materials by C. Lynn Fox, Ph. D.

- *Communicating to Make Friends, Grades K - 6*
- *Creating Drug-Free Schools and Communities: A Comprehensive Approach* college textbook (coauthored with Shirley E. Forbing)
- *Handicapped . . . How Does It Feel, Grades K - 8*
- *Handicapped . . . How Does It Feel, Grades 5 - 12*
- *Project CODE: Collaborating on Drug Education* (coauthored with Jeanne Mendoza, Shirley Forbing, and Karen Knab)
- *Project STOP: Standing Together to Offer Prevention in Drug Education* (coauthored with Shirley E. Forbing)
- *Social Acceptance: Key to Mainstreaming* (coauthored with Ida Malian)
- *Unlocking Doors to Friendship, Grades 7 - 12* (coauthored with Francine Lavin Weaver)

Grades K - 6

Activities for Developing Friendship and Self-Esteem in the Elementary Grades

Affiliation/Belongingness Techniques that Work

C. Lynn Fox, Ph.D.

JP

Jalmar Press
Rolling Hills Estates, California

Let's Get Together!
Activities for Developing Friendship and Self-Esteem in the Elementary Grades K-6

Jalmar Press
Permissions Dept.
Skypark Business Center
2675 Skypark Drive, Suite 204
Torrance, CA 90505
(310) 784-0016 FAX: (310) 784-1379

The student poems that appear throughout this book were taken from *Communicating To Make Friends*, B. L. Winch & Associates, 1980. Permission to use this material has been granted by the publisher.

Library of Congress Catalog Data
92-075 715
CIP

Published by Jalmar Press

Let's Get Together
Activities for Developing Friendship and Self-Esteem in the Elementary Grades K-6

Author: C. Lynn Fox, Ph.D.
Project Director: Janet Lovelady
Artist: Kelly McMahon
Production Consultants: Jeanne Iler & Matthew F. Lopez
Cover Design: Mario A. Artavia II

Manufactured in the United States of America
First edition printing: 10 9 8 7 6 5 4 3 2 1
ISBN 0-915190-75-3

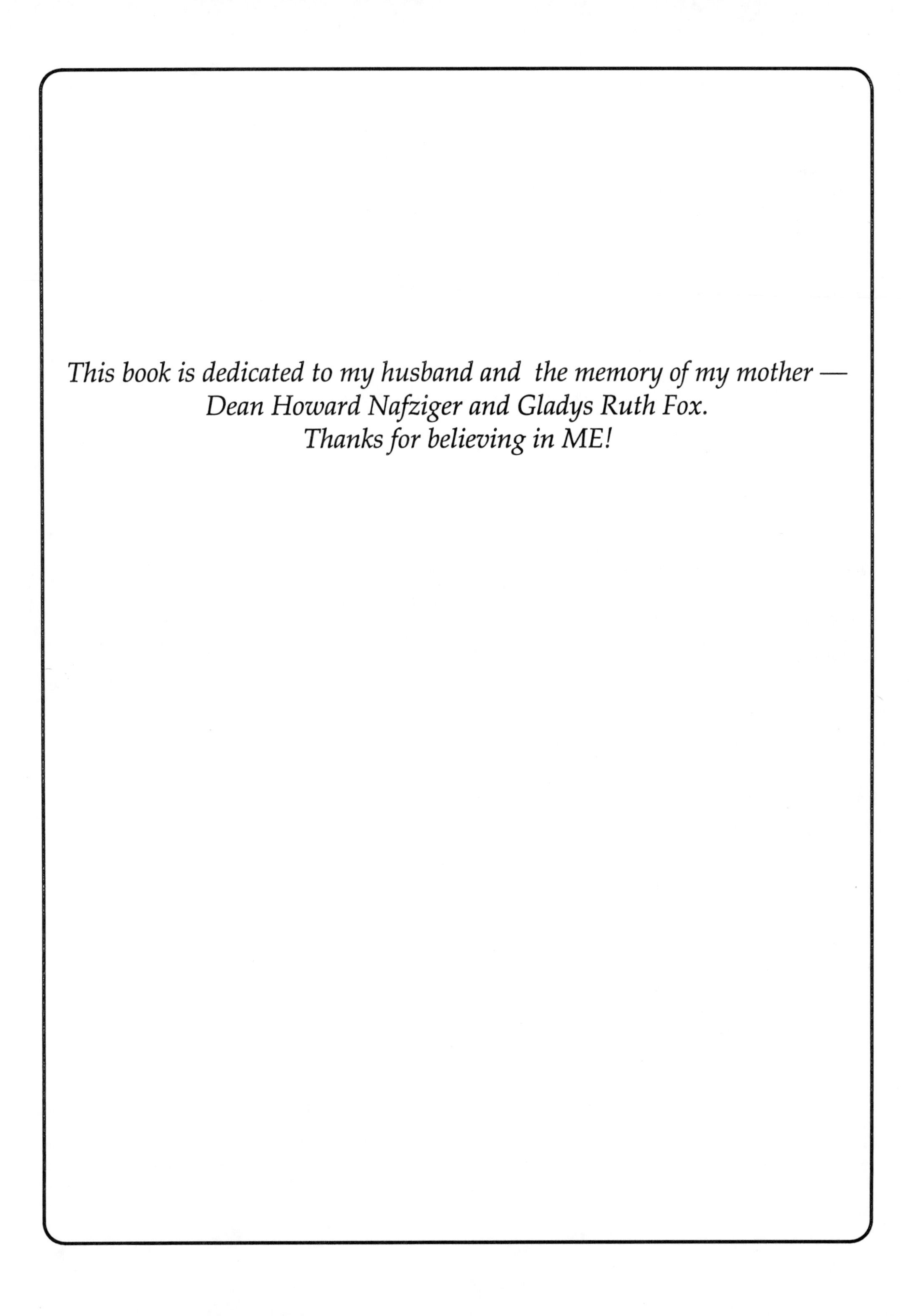

This book is dedicated to my husband and the memory of my mother —
Dean Howard Nafziger and Gladys Ruth Fox.
Thanks for believing in ME!

Acknowledgements

I would like to acknowledge the following professionals and friends for their help:

- Janet Lovelady for her helpful input in editing and designing the book.
- Dr. Bradley Winch for giving me encouragement and support.
- Jane Brucker for her poetry, creativity and kindness.
- Gene Brucker for his efforts in finding poems for the book.
- Students in the San Diego Unified School District who contributed poems.
- Teachers throughout the United States who gave me specific feedback for lessons included in this book.
- Bob, Wreva, and Vanessa Mobley for their creative input on the multicultural activities.
- Dr. Owen Knox, Los Angeles Unified School District Area Supt., Retired, for his support with my research efforts.
- Children in the Los Angeles Unified School District who helped me field test the ideas in the book.
- Dr. Harry Wall for giving me professional support in my research.
- Dr. Jim Duggins, Department of Secondary Education at San Francisco State University for contributing and reviewing the lists of children's books for K - 6 graders.
- Jennifer Merrill Palethorpe for her support with the compilation of materials.
- Student teachers at San Diego State University and their master teachers at Kennedy Elementary School in the San Diego Unified School District for their implementation ideas, practical enrichment activities, and suggestions.
- Kelly McMahon for her delightful artwork.
- Gayla Slikas for her friendship and editing support.

Table of Contents

Research Validation for *Let's Get Together!*

Dr. C. Lynn Fox has been involved in research in the area of friendship building, self-esteem enhancement, and social acceptance since the mid 1970's when she was working on her doctorate at the University of California, Los Angeles. The original research for her first book, *Communicating To Make Friends,* was a two year study done between 1976 and 1978 in the Los Angeles Unified School District in six culturally and linguistically diverse elementary schools. The results of her study were included in a document entitled *Peer Acceptance of Exceptional Children in the Regular Classroom* published in 1979. The purpose of the study was to investigate whether the nature of the social contact between learning disabled children and their nondisabled peers affects the level of peer acceptance for either child, but particularly for the disabled child. The results showed that it is necessary for teachers to do a social intervention with disabled children or their acceptance level will decrease as the school year progresses. Pairing children to discover and discuss mutual interests was found to be the best approach to increase their social acceptance and to help them develop friendships.

From 1980-1989, as a professor at San Diego State University, Dr. Fox continued her research with hundreds of elementary teachers and their diverse student populations using activities from her book *Communicating To Make Friends.* Results continued to show gains in social acceptance and friendship with a minimum of three lessons being done. Teachers throughout the United States supplied additional testimonials to the success of her work.

In 1990 and 1991, Dr. Fox compiled the thousands of pieces of new data which lead to the writing of *Let's Get Together!* At the request of teachers using her research and materials, Dr. Fox included hundreds of exciting and creative activities for incorporating multicultural activities into the academic curriculum. She also found that children's literature could reinforce the social concepts of her research. Thus, she has listed books appropriate for the eighteen lesson topics for both primary and intermediate elementary students.

In order to help Dr. Fox continue her research, please share your ideas as to what worked and new ideas you've tried. Please complete the form on page 178 and return to Dr. Fox. (Address information given on form.)

Introduction

Overview

Every teacher knows the helpless feeling of watching while a child who has been excluded by the other students sits at the edge of a group — the lonely outsider. This kind of social rejection is a stigma that often fuels low self-esteem, which in turn causes negative internalization that can last a lifetime. Not only is the child affected, but in a larger sense and a more long-term scope, all of society — as evidenced in problems such as gang warfare, drug abuse, family dysfunction, and child abuse.

During the last decade, significant changes in the demographic profile of our nation's school population have increasingly intensified the social dynamics in the classroom, so much so that today the lack of understanding and acceptance between students of differing backgrounds and cultures have become the basis for violent and tragic clashes as these youngsters enter the teen years.

There is an urgent need for programs that promote the acceptance of others and the ability to value the self-worth of the individual. The valuable learning experience which comes from understanding people of different backgrounds, colors, and abilities will be lost unless the teacher can somehow encourage all the students in the classroom to positively interact.

Let's Get Together! can make a difference. This book provides a step-by-step program that makes it comfortable and easy for students to learn to get along. Numerous communication, art, and writing activities allow students to become better acquainted in a nonthreatening stressfree environment. By the end of the program, friendship and acceptance are natural outcomes.

The Lonely Outsider

Let's examine more closely the students who may be socially

pted to understand how *Let's* *gether!* can help. There are ...ny categories of students who may be socially rejected by their classmates. Here are a few:

- learning disabled students
- children with physical disabilities
- racially and culturally different students
- youngsters with a language difference
- new students in school
- gifted or regular students with poor social skills
- withdrawn or shy children

It is not uncommon for disabled and handicapped children to be socially rejected. Whether they suffer from physical defects, behavioral disorders, communication difficulties, or learning problems, these students usually have a much harder time making friends.

Until 1975, regular classroom teachers did not have the challenge of mainstreaming these children into the classroom. Children with moderate or severe problems were isolated from the general school population. The enactment of *Public Law 94-142* changed all that. The law required schools to educate handicapped children in "the least restrictive environment," which in many cases meant the regular classroom.

On July 26, 1992 the *Americans With Disabilities Act* (PL 101-336) further reinforced the rights of all disabled individuals. While both laws provide important protection for handicapped students and adults, they have given schools the added responsibility of making sure the entire classroom adjusts socially and accepts diversities.

At the same time, racially and culturally different children have been appearing in classrooms in record numbers due to shifts in the population and the implementation of mandatory integration programs. These children often enter the school at a disadvantage not only because of language differences, but also because the other students have already established their friendships and social cliques.

Consider the new child who moves into the neighborhood in the middle of the year. Most of the other students have already established their friendships based on common experiences not just from that school year, but from a long-term association with each other. It is very difficult for the new student to break into the established social circle. The neighborhood pupils see the new student as an outsider and, as is natural for children, view his or her differences — cultural or racial — as undesirable. These differences need to be addressed early on, before they escalate into tension and deadly conflict.

Another area of concern is with the students in class who are gifted. These children often have trouble making friends for two reasons. Either their peers resent the intellectual superiority of these children or, as is more often the case, gifted students become so focused on academics that their social skills remain undeveloped. These students may not be asked to join classmates at lunch, during recess, or in after-school games, so they miss out on opportunities to interact with others.

It's the same situation for the shy, withdrawn students who don't take the initiative when looking for friends. Unfortunately, popular students feel they have very little reason to try and draw these classmates out, so the shy students remain isolated.

Social skills are every bit as important to survival in the adult world as academic or physical abilities. Some children develop social skills naturally, others have to be coached. This program will help any students who are not as skilled at making friends as their classmates and at the same time, enhance the social skills of the whole class. The self-esteem of each student will be strengthened.

How to Help

We've all seen the serious problems that can evolve from social isolation. Loss of self-esteem and many behavioral problems begin when a child feels rejected. There are three important actions teachers can take to change this syndrome:

- Project an accepting attitude and become a positive model for the students.

- Help change the child's inappropriate social behavior.

- Help change the attitude of the child's classmates.

The most successful approach is to incorporate all three actions in the process. As a first step, it is quite natural for educators to want to build a caring and nurturing environment in the classroom. The chapter on *The Teacher as a Model* will provide some additional ideas to enrich understanding in this area.

Many teachers make diligent efforts to change the social behavior of the unaccepted student by using coaching, shaping, or modeling methods. However, even when they are successful at affecting the individual child's behavior, educators are still ith the need to change the es of the rest of the class ards the unaccepted child — a much more challenging task.

That's where *Let's Get Together!* comes in. This program, which is researched-based and student-tested in hundreds of classrooms throughout the country, is designed to change the whole social climate in the classroom. The activities will widen each student's realm of relationships while teaching valuable lessons in interpersonal involvements along with academic skills.

Teachers have found that by using this process to change their students' attitudes, less time and training are actually required than by trying solely to change the unaccepted child's behavior. While participating in the program, the unaccepted child will grow by imitating the more acceptable social behaviors of his or her peers.

Program Background

Youngsters are attracted to others with similarities. But unless they sit down and talk, they'll never know what they have in common. Just putting two students together does not guarantee the necessary exchange of ideas, values, and feelings. The lessons in *Let's Get Together!* are especially designed to help students discover and discuss their common background experiences, interests, and feelings.

To understand the principles involved in social acceptance, it is important to examine the theory and research concerning why people like one another or are attracted to each other. There are two important friendship research theories that explain why the focus of this book is on the discovery and discussion of similar personal experiences, interests, and feelings.

The first approach is the Cognitive Balance Theory which analyzes the ways in which two individuals relate. The second approach is referred to as the Reinforcement Theory, which explains why positive social relationships develop when similarities are highlighted.

The Cognitive Balance Theory deals with three types of interactions that can take place between two individuals when they are evaluating a common person, action, or thing. The first kind of interaction is one in which they both have a similar knowledge base and so evaluate the item of discussion in a similar manner. As a result of their similar feelings, the two individuals are bonded into a positive interaction.

The second type of interaction occurs when the two have the same interest but disagree about the value of it. This disagreement creates an imbalance and leads to a negative relationship relative to the focal point of disagreement. If the difference is not resolved, this imbalance will negatively affect the overall relationship.

The third type of interaction that can occur is when two individuals disagree about the value, as well as the evaluation, of the person, action, or thing with which they are dealing. This creates a negative relationship as well.

Let's Get Together! helps students begin their new relationship on a positive note by creating interactions similar to the first one described (i.e. same interest, same evaluation).

As explained by the Reinforcement Theory, the reason positive bonding occurs between two individuals is because they are demonstrating that their relationship is functioning in a logical and meaningful way. This relationship creates a more predictable, stable interpersonal environment and thus allows the friendship to develop naturally.

Opportunities to learn about personal commonalities lead to an increased interest in building a relationship. The activities in this book provide those opportunities for discovery as children explore similarities among themselves.

Program Objectives

Here are the specific objectives of the program:

- To help every student understand emotions.
- To help every student be more understanding and accepting of individual differences.
- To help every student see similarities between themselves and their peers.
- To help every student learn to solve interpersonal problems.
- To help every student learn to share common experiences, interests, and feelings.
- To help every student increase communication skills.

Program Description

The program consists of eighteen weekly lessons for use in the elementary grades. The six holiday lessons are optional (Lessons 9, 12, 15, 16, 17, 18). Students work in pairs to create Partner Books about each other. Specific instructions for determining how students should be paired are discussed on pages 10 - 16.

The lessons in *Let's Get Together!* are designed to follow the natural flow of a friendship. There are three

...nt stages in the development ...ationship, each one more ...ding:

- **Stage I — Talking Over Facts**
- **Stage II — Discussing Interests**
- **Stage III — Sharing Feelings**

Stage I - Lessons 1 to 5 focus on letting the children get to know one another. The youngsters begin the relationship with their partners by discovering and discussing mutual *facts* (or background experiences) about each other.

Stage II - Lessons 6 to 10 provide many opportunities for the students to share *interests.* This is the next normal stage of development. As the participants begin to discover interests they share, it is quite natural for a closer bond to form.

Stage III - Lessons 11 to 18 allow students to talk about their *feelings* — both good and bad. At this point in the program, the partners are more likely to open up and share their opinions and emotions because they have learned to feel comfortable with each other.

Each lesson takes approximately one hour to complete, depending on the skills of the students. The activities can be incorporated into the classroom in a variety of ways:

- Pair the children and have them work on the assignments weekly. (If an hour is too long, divide the lessons into thirty-minute sessions and do them twice a week.)

- Have an instructional aide or volunteer work with small groups on the project. (The highly-structured nature of this program makes it easy for a volunteer to administer.) If an aide or volunteer can spend half a day in the classroom, the students can be divided into three groups of approximately five pairs each. The rest of the students can do a regular lesson with the teacher or independent work from their regular academic schedule.

- Use the lessons as a weekly art, language, and writing assignment. All of the children would be involved at the same time. The artwork activities are designed to produce immediate success for the students — an important part of building self-worth.

If possible, it is best to implement the program during the first semester of the school year. The longer a teacher waits, the harder it is to change the negative attitudes students develop towards the unaccepted children. However, if the program can't be started early in the year, it will still be very beneficial, whenever it is begun.

It is important to allow enough time for the students to complete at least eight lessons; however, the most effective results will come from the completion of the entire program.

Program Components

Each lesson is comprised of these elements:

- Background information.
- Enrichment and multicultural activities for whole class involvement.
- A reading list of appropriate children's literature to enhance the focus of the lesson and help students examine the feelings and challenges of other young people.
- A four-part reproducible student lesson activity.

Children follow the four-part activity of each lesson in a sequential manner, always beginning with an interview. The first page of the student section in each lesson provides interview questions. The questions help the children find out information about each other, pertinent to the theme of the lesson.

The interview activity is meant to be a verbal exchange. A minimum of writing is needed on this page and the questionnaires should be returned to the teacher when the children have completed the lesson. The second page of the student section in each lesson gives the directions for the art activity and the third page is a prepared artwork project. The artwork activities give the children a chance to evaluate and think about what they have learned from each other.

The art activities were designed and have been tested to prevent a discrepancy between the two partners' artistic abilities. This is especially important when one of the partners has a learning disability such as poor fine motor skills and/or poor eye-hand coordination.

The fourth page provides several poems written by other youngsters and directs the children to create their own poems, stories, riddles, songs, and commercials.

The Interviewing Technique

Having students interview each other is the most direct way possible to get them to discuss mutual experiences, interests, and feelings. The interview questions in each lesson are designed specifically to elicit similar answers from the students. On each questionnaire the students are asked to list three things the partners have in common with each other.

An elementary school pilot test for this program showed that most students gave similar answers to ninety percent of the questions. The study revealed that the partners had no difficulty finding at least three things in each interview which they both shared as experiences, interests, goals, values, or feelings.

The interviewing technique gives the teacher more control over the interaction of the partners than allowing them to make up their own questions. It sets the program in a realistic time frame which allows it to be easily implemented into the regular classroom curriculum. It is important for the teacher to read the interview questions aloud to the students first.

If possible, assign the best reader in the partner grouping to conduct the interview first. This will make it easier for the poor reader when it is time for that student to read the questions. After they complete the questionnaire, the students should be encouraged to discuss and ask their own questions, as long as they stay on the topic of the lessons.

A more detailed discussion of the interviewing process is included in the Lesson 1 background information. Make sure the partners understand their time limits and know that they must complete their interviews within the predetermined time frame. Allow for longer time periods during the first few lessons.

The only writing that the children are required to do for the interview is to put checkmarks beside specific questions when requested and to complete the three blanks at the bottom of the questionnaire page. The three blanks can be completed with sentences, phrases, words, or illustrations, depending on the ability of the children.

Partner Books

The completed artwork and writing sheets should be compiled and placed into a Partner Book. The interview sheets are not meant to be put into the books, although they *can* be included if the students and teacher are comfortable with this idea. Each personalized Partner Book will tell something about the partner's experiences, interests, and feelings.

If appropriate, ask the students to use pencils for the writing portions of the assignments, have their spelling checked by an adult, and trace the final work with a thin-line marker. The Partner Books will be more organized if the students' pages are stored in one place during the year instead of trying to let the children keep track of their own papers.

After the partners have finished the contents of their Partner Books, it would be appropriate for them to design and decorate book covers. The covers can be made from cardboard, construction paper, or regular paper. Colorful yarn could be used to bind the pages together. The students can use crayons, marking pens, paint, and glitter to decorate their book covers in any way they choose. Let the children be as creative as they want.

Another idea for the cover would be to have the children trace their partners' names on colorful construction paper, cut out the letters, and paste them to the fronts of the Partner Books. Often the children ask their partners what type of design they would like on the cover of the book. *As a ready-to-go alternative, two reproducible pages that can be used as front and back covers for the Partner Books are included at the end of Lesson 18.*

Holiday Lessons

Among the eighteen lessons, there are six lessons which deal specifically with holidays that occur during the school year: Halloween, Thanksgiving, Christmas and Hanukkah, Valentine's Day, Birthdays, and Spring Vacation.

The holiday lessons are included because it is quite common for students to talk about the celebrations and festivities associated with these special occasions, and so they already have a common interest that they can share. The teacher may choose to use the holidays lessons as part of the special event instead of looking for other projects.

Many holidays really do personify what the program is trying to teach students. Halloween and Birthdays are perhaps the most exciting days of the year for students. It should be easy to get them talking to each other about tricks and treats or birthday surprises — and before they know it, they may be friends.

Thanksgiving and Valentine's Day are good times to start discussing the interests and feelings which naturally evolve during these holidays. Christmas and Hanukkah are times when students often will be feeling joy and/or sadness. By using these holidays as a springboard for discussion, the teacher will discover an excellent opportunity to help the children deal with these powerful emotions.

If the program is implemented in the fall semester, the Halloween, Thanksgiving, and Christmas/Hanukkah lessons would be the logical lessons to use. During the spring semester, the Valentine's Day, Birthday, and Spring Vacation lessons would be more appropriate.

Program Management

Because this program is so valuable to the establishment of a positive social environment in the classroom, it is important that the lessons run smoothly. The following management ideas might be of help:

- Never assume a child has prerequisite skills for a prescribed task.

- Be precise. Specificity in objectives is *very* important.
- Encourage each student to be an *active* partner so progress will occur.
- Provide structure.
- Promote a predictable learning environment.
- Try to minimize extraneous stimuli.
- Be versatile — match the most suitable method and materials with the student's needs. Inflexibility should be avoided.
- Use visuals, peer tutoring, one-on-one, large or small groups, programmed instruction.
- Pace instruction appropriately.
- Provide plenty of examples so a new concept or activity will be thoroughly understood and not leave the students feeling frustrated.
- Monitor student performance frequently.
- Speed up or slow down the lesson based on student performance.

Program Modifications

As with any program developed for a large population of users, teachers need to be able to modify and adjust it to meet their own time frames, student needs, and resources.

It is possible to make changes in the lessons as long as teachers keep in mind the primary goals of the overall focus of the program: to help children make friends and discover their self-worth. Here are a few suggestions for modifying the program:

- Let the students ask fewer questions during the interview.
- Have the students use a typewriter or computer to answer the questions.
- Ask the students to use a tape recorder to complete the interview.
- Allow students who find it difficult to draw, cut out pictures from magazines or catalogs instead.
- Delete the writing portion on the art page by placing a strip of blank paper over this section before making copies for the class.

How to Pair Students

Students are assigned a partner of the same sex, whom they work with for the duration of the program. If some children do not seem to be working well together and a change is being considered, it is important that the partner-switching not be made until at least five lessons are completed. It usually takes at least three lessons to change negative feelings and it is best to give the students some time to adjust to each other before a final decision is made.

It is recommended that the partners be the same sex, since research indicates that elementary students feel more comfortable working with students of the same gender. The enrichment and multicultural activities described at the end of the teacher's section for each lesson will provide ample opportunities for the whole class to interact without regard to sexual differences.

It is very important to pair accepted students with unaccepted youngsters. Children make up their minds very quickly about classmates they like and don't like, so you will be able to observe who the most popular students are and who is left out very early in the school year.

There are two methods for determining partner groupings — the formal and the informal procedure. Both types have been included in this book. *The forms on pages 14 - 16 may be reproduced for classroom purposes.* If a formal approach is desired, the Friendship Survey and Form A can be used. The Friendship Survey needs to be filled out by the students in class. Then the survey results are recorded and tallied on Form A by the teacher.

If a more informal technique is appropriate, use Form B. Regardless of the method used, it is important that the partners not be randomly assigned. The whole purpose of the program is to help those who do not accept each other to learn to get along.

Assessment Procedure

Formal Approach

Make two copies of the Friendship Survey. Write the names of male students on one copy and female students on the other. Make copies of each list and distribute the list of males to the boys and the list of females to the girls.

Ask the children to write their own names at the top of the surveys and have them rate each classmate on the list with a number from one to six. They will enter the numbers in both of the columns and answer the questions:

- How much do you like to play with this person?
- How much do you like to work with this person?

Tell the students to write the numbers next to the student's name, under the appropriate column on the form. The rating scores of one to six points represent acceptance levels.

- One point should be given for: "I don't like to at all."
- Two points should be given for: "I don't like to."
- Three points should be given for: "I sort of don't like to."
- Four points should be given for: "I sort of like to."
- Five points should be given for: "I like to."
- Six points should be given for: "I like to very much."

Make sure that the children understand the difference between the six categories. Number one can be explained as the rating a student would give to a child he or she would never choose to play with. Number two would be given to a classmate who the student might play with if forced to by the teacher but would probably be someone the student would end up fighting.

Number three stands for the classmate that the student might want to play with, but not if someone more compatible was around. Number four is the rating a student would give to a classmate that is fun to be with most of the time, and number five is for the classmate that the student chooses to play with a lot.

Number six is the rating the students should use only for those few special friends with whom they always like to play. If the student was choosing a team, he or she would want to pick the number sixes first. It would be helpful to select some popular entertainers, sports figures, or cartoon characters to illustrate the rating system. After the students have completed the Friendship Survey, use Form A to tally the ratings and average them for an overall score.

EXAMPLE: From one student, Mary receives a three for "play with" and a five for "work with." Her score from that classmate is a four. Add this score to Mary's other scores to get an average, or a class score, for her. Use Mary's class score to compare her with the other females in class and find her relative ranking.

Next, add up the total mean scores (ratings given by every same-sexed classmate) and find the individual's average class score. Use this number to rank all of the students from high to low.

Students ranked in the top half of the class should be paired with students who are in the lower half of the rankings. Check the ratings of possible partners and make sure that they are not highly accepting of each other. Two students who gave each other sixes should not be paired. Try to pair partners who gave each other rankings of three or four.

Look closely at the accepted student's rating of the isolated student. This is usually a better indicator of the true rating of a student, since the unaccepted children tend to give other students much higher overall scores.

It may be difficult to find a classmate the unaccepted student has rated low. That's because the isolated student wants so badly to be a part of the crowd. If this occurs, pair the children according to the popular student's rating of the unaccepted child. Consider the personalities of the students being matched. If pairing two children is going to cause behavior problems and require an undue amount of discipline time, the benefits of the program will be lost.

If a teacher is confident that through behavior management training the problems can be overcome, it may be worthwhile to pair the two students. Just be sure to consider each case carefully. Avoid pairing two students whose academic achievement varies greatly. This can create a barrier between the partners, which will defeat the purpose of the program before they have had a chance to get to know each other. When introducing the program to the class, explain that the pairing was made as fairly as possible and that no one can change partners, because it would affect the whole program. Play down the process of pairing and focus on the purpose of the project.

Emphasize that each student is going to have a book written about him or her by a partner and that the Partner Books can be given to anyone the class chooses. (Lesson 1 explains the reasons for making the book in more detail and offers suggestions for recipients.)

Informal Approach

Make several copies of Form B, depending on the number of students in class. Separate the students' names by gender, setting up a list for the boys and a list for the girls.

Put a check in any column 1 - 7 that is applicable to the students. The code box for the checking system is at the top of Form B. Column eight should be used to list any classmates who have had positive interaction with the student. The list in column eight does not need to be extensive.

It will become quickly obvious which students have more social needs than others by the number of checkmarks in columns 1 - 7. Pair students who have extra needs with children who have fewer checkmarks.

Friendship Survey

Put a number in both columns for each student. Use the rating box.

Name ______________________________

RATING BOX

1 = I don't like to at all
2 = I don't like to
3 = I sort of don't like to
4 = I sort of like to
5 = I like to
6 = I like to very much

Names of Classmates	Play With	Work With
1.		
2.		
3.		
4.		
5.		
6.		
7.		
8.		
9.		
10.		
11.		
12.		
13.		
14.		
15.		
16.		
17.		

Names of Classmates	Play With	Work With
18.		
19.		
20.		
21.		
22.		
23.		
24.		
25.		
26.		
27.		
28.		
29.		
30.		
31.		
32.		
33.		
34.		

Form A: Formal Record

Use the Friendship Survey to tally all the student ratings and average them for an overall score.

Names of BOYS	Class Avg.	Class Rank
1.		
2.		
3.		
4.		
5.		
6.		
7.		
8.		
9.		
10.		
11.		
12.		
13.		
14.		
15.		
16.		
17.		
18.		
19.		
20.		

Names of GIRLS	Class Avg.	Class Rank
1.		
2.		
3.		
4.		
5.		
6.		
7.		
8.		
9.		
10.		
11.		
12.		
13.		
14.		
15.		
16.		
17.		
18.		
19.		
20.		

Form B: Informal Record

a) List all students in your class by sex, alphabetically.
b) Put a check in any column 1 - 7 that is applicable to each student.
c) List classmates in column 8 who have had positive interaction with the student.

Column # 1 = Loner	Column # 4 = Lingers after class
Column # 2 = Usually at the end of the line	Column # 5 = Presents behavioral problem in class
Column # 3 = Usually breaks into lines or groups	Column # 6 = Seeks to be with younger aged children
	Column # 7 = Seeks older aged students or adults

Student Names	1	2	3	4	5	6	7	8

The Teacher as a Model

Overview

A major focus of any school program should be the fostering of positive self-esteem in the classroom and the development of better social relationships among all students. Teachers need to commit themselves to the implementation of specific goals in the social needs areas, with the same urgency that they give to creating a sound academic curriculum or physical education program.

The best place to implement a change in the classroom is to begin with a evaluation of one's own actions and feelings. Because a teacher is one of the most significant people in the students' lives, it is important to find out whether or not the educator's influence is being used to the greatest advantage in the classroom.

It is important to know that it is not what is *said* that students act upon, but instead what is *done*. About 65% of all communication is accomplished through actions and body language.

When a teacher models both self-confidence and an acceptance of all students, this attitude is mirrored by the children. It becomes easier for students to express a similar viewpoint.

The self-assessment instrument on pages 21 - 23 will be helpful for evaluation purposes. It allows the teacher to find out what is being positively modeled and where new approaches are needed. Pages 24 - 26 are helpful reminders for teachers to use on a daily basis.

There are many classroom activities that will provide a positive, motivating, and successful experience for each student. These three areas are important to focus on: *praise, respect,* and *effective communication.*

Praise

It would be helpful to take time to find out about your students' interests and hobbies. Find out from them what activities they are involved in outside school hours. One child might like to play computer games, while another could be good at horseback riding or dancing. Information about students will help the teacher "spice up" the curriculum or provide opportunities to compliment a child by showing a thoughtful interest in his or her accomplishments. Children get excited when they know a teacher values their skills, talents, or interests and most will be pleased when compliments are shared with the whole class.

Many teachers use inventories, questionnaires, or surveys to find out about specific interests. The goal is to be aware that all students can excel at something. Here are some additional ways to offer praise.

1. Look for things each child does well and discuss these accomplishments in a meaningful way.

2. Provide assignments in which the students have a choice. For example they can be given a choice of mediums to use in expressing their answer to a problem (e.g. through poetry, art, speech, or in written prose).

3. Break down tasks into simple steps, which allow students to find success in the various steps needed to accomplish a specific goal. This will motivate children to continue an assignment.

4. Use small group activities so shy students feel less intimidated. These children will have more of a chance to participate and thus discover they know more than they originally thought.

5. Grade students on improvement and effort. Portfolio grading is another good option. Students can choose the assignments on which they want to be graded.

6. Create a noncompetitive and cooperative learning atmosphere by giving all students a sense of responsibility.

7. Let students know your expectations, both academic and behavioral, before they start a task.

8. Assign tasks that have open-ended solutions and no one right answer.

9. Give all students the chance to be the "leader" of a group or learning situation.

10. Applaud effort and successful experiences.

11. Have award ceremonies from time to time.

12. Call home for good behavior. Focus on two to three students a week until you've called all the

children's parents.

13. Allow students to retake tests with the possibility of improving their scores.

Respect

In order for students to act respectful toward their teachers and other classmates, they need to see respect modeled in the classroom. There are many ways a teacher can show how respect is achieved.

1. Keep high expectations for all students and work with individual children to help them reach those expectations.

2. Model empathy, rather than pity or sympathy.

3. Ask students about their opinions and follow through with their suggestions, if possible.

4. Don't allow public put-downs.

5. Ask students to give feedback on your performance as a teacher. Respect their input and use it to improve your teaching.

6. Be consistent and treat all students fairly.

7. Let students help to teach the class.

8. Foster appreciation for cultural differences by letting culturally diverse students share their ideas and customs.

9. Help students make their own decisions, rather than waiting for the teacher to tell them what to do.

10. Have a "student of the week" award in which each student is acknowledged for things that are unique about him or her.

11. Develop a welcoming committee for new students in the class. Children can develop ways to make new students feel a part of the group.

12. Teach students about various cultures, races, languages, disabilities, and sexes. Help the children become aware of the similarities and the uniquenesses of each group.

Effective Communication

As teachers improve their own communication skills, this will lead to students being more effective communicators. One very important strategy is to practice active listening.

Another method is to teach students how to give feedback in a manner which is nonthreatening and conveys a real concern for the individual. A book entitled *Teacher Effectiveness Training (T.E.T.)* written by Thomas Gordon, is an excellent source for learning good communication skills.

Teachers can also influence their students positively by showing them that they are people, as well as teachers. Students appreciate it when teachers share who they are, what they like and dislike, their strengths, and areas that they feel need improvement. Some communication ideas that can be incorporated into the teaching day are:

1. Have equal sharing time for all students and yourself.

2. Hold personal conferences with the students to find out what they think and want for themselves.

3. Ask students to express their opinions.

4. Make positive personal comments to celebrate your students' uniquenesses.

5. Teach children to be problem solvers and nonjudgmental about their classmates.

6. Allow students time to disclose how they feel about things that are happening in the classroom and in the school.

7. Use your voice and verbal interactions with students in a positive way.

8. Never act as if any question is stupid.

9. Clarify appropriate versus inappropriate behavior rather than immediately punishing a student who has made a mistake.

10. Train students to actively listen to others.

11. Give honest praise.

12. Be flexible on days when student morale is low or when physical ailments are present.

13. Provide time for students to write in nongraded journals.

Teacher as a Model: Self-Assessment

Directions:
To evaluate your skills as a good model for your students, complete the following assessment.

To what extent as a teacher do I . . .

	not at all	somewhat	to a great extent
PRAISE			
1. Create opportunities that facilitate success.	1	2	3
2. Demonstrate an attitude of acceptance toward students.	1	2	3
3. Allow students to be helpers.	1	2	3
4. Convey a feeling of acceptance that it is OK to make mistakes.	1	2	3
5. Write positive comments on students' work.	1	2	3
6. Look for the strengths of the slower students.	1	2	3
7. Require work that is within the range of each student's ability.	1	2	3
8. Provide praise in a sincere manner.	1	2	3

From: *Social Acceptance: Key to Mainstreaming* by C. Lynn Fox and Ida M. Malian, B. L. Winch & Associates, Rolling Hills Estates, CA., 1983, pp 5-9.

Teacher as a Model: Self-Assessment - page 2

To what extent as a teacher do I . . .

	not at all	somewhat	to a great extent
9. Demonstrate that I value and accept individual differences in the students.	1	2	3
10. Set realistic expectations for students, not too low or too high.	1	2	3
RESPECT			
1. Deal with and attempt to resolve my own frustrations.	1	2	3
2. Empathize with my students, rather than pity or sympathize with them.	1	2	3
3. Appreciate and try to understand each student's own beliefs.	1	2	3
4. Project a feeling of genuineness in interaction with the students.	1	2	3
5. Facilitate the students' feelings of uniqueness.	1	2	3
6. Provide both formal and informal feedback relating to behavior, through private and semiprivate conversations with the students.	1	2	3

From: *Social Acceptance: Key to Mainstreaming* by C. Lynn Fox and Ida M. Malian, B. L. Winch & Associates, Rolling Hills Estates, CA., 1983, pp 5-9.

Teacher as a Model: Self-Assessment - page 3

To what extent as a teacher do I . . .

EFFECTIVE COMMUNICATION	not at all	somewhat	to a great extent
1. Share my own feelings and thoughts with my students.	1	2	3
2. Encourage students to openly relate their feelings.	1	2	3
3. Convey to the students that everyone has strengths *and* improvement areas.	1	2	3
4. Really listen to what the students have to say, rather than telling them what they should think.	1	2	3
5. Acknowledge that I have heard what a student is saying.	1	2	3
6. Smile and show other methods of nonverbal acceptance.	1	2	3
7. Demonstrate to students who return after an absence that I am happy to have them back, and that they were missed.	1	2	3
8. Avoid treating students as either "pets" or "pests."	1	2	3

From: *Social Acceptance: Key to Mainstreaming* by C. Lynn Fox and Ida M. Malian, B. L. Winch & Associates, Rolling Hills Estates, CA., 1983, pp 5-9.

Keeping the Day on a Positive Track

Positive comments reinforce good work. Students will try harder if they feel good about what they have accomplished.

Unfortunately when the same comment is repeated too many times, it becomes trite and no longer reinforcing. Here is a list of positive track statements which will not only communicate to the student that he or she is worthy, but also give your compliments a sense of freshness each day.

- Good for you!
- Thanks for starting your work.
- You're on the right track.
- Hurray! You did it!
- Thanks for making my day.
- Super duper!
- Great job!
- I'm proud of you.
- Well done.
- Good thinking.
- You are tops!
- Congratulations.
- Keep up the good work.
- A different approach!
- You've really got it.
- WOW!
- Exceptional work.
- Perfect!
- Something special.
- You're something else!
- OK!
- Well organized.
- You've accomplished what you set out to do.
- Absolutely the best you've done today.
- I like how you did your (math, reading, art, etc.) because you . . .
- Very creative.
- You've put a lot of work into this.
- Clever idea!
- You've got a good start.
- It's fun to read your papers.
- You've put a lot of thought into this.
- You're pretty special!
- Beautiful!
- Outstanding.
- You've done ten neat things today.
- It's a pleasure to have you in class.
- I'm glad you're here today.
- Very perceptive!
- Nicely done.
- You've come a long way.
- You are a crackerjack!
- DY-NO-MITE!
- Sensational!
- That's really good.
- Unbelievable.
- I like this point.
- Well organized.
- Keep going! You're headed in the right direction!
- I look forward to seeing you tomorrow.
- It's good to have you back.
- I appreciate what you have to say.

From: *Social Acceptance: Key to Mainstreaming* by C. Lynn Fox and Ida M. Malian, B. L. Winch & Associates, Rolling Hills Estates, CA., 1983, pp 5-9.

PRAISE: An Approach to Effective Learning

Praise

Students need to know when they have done well and to hear it in a positive, novel manner. Utilize the list of positive track statements when communicating with children.

Reason

Students also need to know why they are being praised. Not only does this facilitate the likelihood of future occurrence of this behavior, but it models the desired skill.

Approval

When you review the students' papers, voice your approval of both the completed work, and the manner in which the work was done. Approval of individual worth should be stressed during all communication.

Improvement

Students should be aware of where they stand in terms of themselves (example: 84 out of 100 correct) and their peers (example: 4 other students received 84 — the highest grade was 94 and the lowest was 64).

Suggestions

Specific comments on how the student can improve, along with examples, should be shared. The teacher can serve as a model for such suggestions. For example, if a student needs to improve organizational skills, the teacher can model his or her techniques of organization. A list or chart of sequential activities can be made available for the students to copy.

Evaluation

At this point, the student should resubmit corrected work. Options for evaluation may include: self-correction, correction by peers, correction between student and teacher. This is an extremely important step in the total procedure. If overlooked, initial errors become consistent errors.

Grading Papers Can Be Meaningful When You . . .

- Use a color of pen other than red. Many students equate red with "bad."

- Place the number correct on the top of the paper. Stress the items that are correct, not the ones that were incorrect.

- Provide a positive statement for items that are done well and provide positive suggestions for improvement for those items that are not correct.

- Distribute criteria for grading prior to doing the grading. Go over the criteria with the students and provide examples.

- Set yourself up as a positive and supportive model for the students, rather than a punisher and judge.

- Highlight the positive aspects of the paper with stars, asterisks, check marks, plus marks, and/or single word comments. (Refer to the list of positive track statements.)

- Pinpoint where the errors are and allow students to correct their mistakes and resubmit for evaluation.

- Separate the performance from the person. Convey to students that the test score or grade reflects knowledge of specific information and NOT personal worth.

Lesson 1: Getting to Know My Partner

Overview and Objectives

Think about the last person you talked to. What was the color of that individual's eyes? Can you describe his or her face? We rarely take time to really look at the people around us. Unfortunately, if someone has a club foot, a cleft-palate lip, a different way of speaking, or an unfamiliar way of dressing, these characteristics may prevent us from noticing the friendliness of a smile or the sparkle in a pair of eyes. We sometimes feel uncomfortable about people we don't understand. Children feel this way too, just as strongly as do adults.

Lesson 1 is designed to help students in the classroom focus on ways they are alike, rather than ways they are different. As students clarify physical similarities and differences, they will see themselves and their partners in a broader context and begin to value the whole person. The activities give the children an opportunity to look carefully at each other without feeling like they are being nosey or discourteous. Though they will find differences, students will also find many similarities.

Getting Started

Since this is the first lesson of the program, it is important to take time to explain it thoroughly.

Purpose

Let the students know that each of them will be working on a Partner Book — a book about another person in the classroom. Impress upon the students that everyone in the class will be involved in the program and that this project will provide them with a good opportunity to get to know each other better. Stress that a completed book is the primary reason for doing the activities.

Make the completion of the book sound like an important achievement. Your students need to know that you think the project is both fun and worthwhile. Explain that the books will be given to whomever the class chooses as recipients such as:

- Younger students in the school so they can read and learn about their older classmates.

- The school library so that each student will be remembered.

- Parents or friends for special holiday gifts.

- The classroom library so class members can read the books during free time and get to know each other better.

You may have your own explanation for this program. Be careful not to imply that your students are doing the activities because you want them to accept partners that no one in the class likes. The purpose is to blend in the unaccepted child, not embarrass that student.

Partner Assignments
Students should feel that you are being as fair as possible about your pairing decisions. Explain that they are being paired with a classmate of the same sex only because there are questions that they may prefer to discuss with someone of their own sex.

Let the students know that they will be paired with others in the class whom they do not know very well. That way the book will be a fun way for them to find out about their classmates. Tell the students that they can't change partners because it would not be fair to the rest of the class.

Point out that the students are reporters and that a reporter doesn't always know the person he or she is going to interview until they have a chance to talk together. Explain that each student will complete a book about his or her partner.

Special Note:
Research indicates that in social situations, elementary school students respond better if they are paired with children of the same sex . Some teachers may feel students would feel comfortable with a partner of the opposite sex. The way you pair your students will depend on the special circumstances in your classroom. The enrichment and multicultural activities in each lesson will provide many opportunities for whole class interaction.

Lesson Format

Let the children know the three basic components of each lesson:

- A one-page interview.

- A two-page art project.

• A one-page writing assignment.

The Interview Activity

Time: 10 - 20 minutes

The interview activity is the most important part of this program. It helps the students discover commonalities. The information on the questionnaires will also help you find out more about the interests of the children in the classroom. This is particularly useful when planning lessons for certain content areas.

Explain what an interview is or have the students look up the definition of the word and discuss it. Ask the children if they've ever seen an interview on television. Use whatever technique you choose to explain how interviews are conducted. Let the students know that written answers are not required except as indicated on the interview page. Allow five to ten minutes for each partner to interview the other.

After the interviews, students discuss at least three things they have in common and write these at the bottom of the interview questionnaire page. Stress the value of the interview activity by explaining that it will help students complete the art and writing activities.

The interview page is to be turned in after the lesson is completed. This page does not need to go in the Partner Book, unless it seems appropriate. Only the completed art activity page (the third student page) and the writing page (the fourth student page) need to be included in the Partner Books.

If you expect behavior problems, structure the sessions and develop rules for interviewing and working together. You may need rules to deal with: deciding who reads the questions first, staying with questions that relate to the topic, handling arguments and loud talking.

The Art Activity

Time: 30 minutes

Each student will need two art pages to complete this exercise. Explain to the children that the first of the two art pages includes a list of materials needed to complete the project, as well as directions and illustrations for cutting and pasting.

Tell the class that the directions on the first art page will tell them how to complete a drawing of their partner's face on the second art page. They will also color in their partner's hair, eyes, and clothes.

At the bottom of the second art page, the students will write two simple sentences that tell something about their partner's appearance. Remind the children that only *positive* qualities should be listed. The sentences should focus on the person being interviewed and not on the person who is writing. Examples of sentences could be put on the board for younger children, but older students should be encouraged to write their own ideas.

If the Partner Books are going to be shared with younger students or if there are students in class who have trouble reading and writing cursive, ask the children to print the sentences in manuscript lettering.

Explain that most books are printed in manuscript. This explanation will prevent embarrassment should there be students in class who have learning problems.

If appropriate, you should encourage the students to use pencils for writing so misspellings can be corrected. Then the corrected sentences can be traced with a black thin-tip marking pen. Since this is an optional approach, the list of materials does not include a black marking pen.

The Writing Activity

Time: 30 minutes

The writing page includes poems written by other students. Ask the partners to read the poems aloud to each other and then write a poem of their own. If appropriate, use the same writing suggestions discussed under the art activity.

Interview Session Script

Here is a script that may be used when presenting the first interviewing session:

You will be interviewing each other and making picture/word books about your partner. Who knows what an interview is? (Explain and discuss.)

Each week you will have a new topic to discuss with your partner. Many times in school, students are asked to write a book about themselves. This time you will interview your partner and create a book about that person, not about yourself. While interviewing each other, see if you can find three things that you both have in common such as: Were you both born in the same state?

(Ask if there are any questions, then continue.)

Here are a few ideas to get you started.

(Introduce the topic for Lesson 1 and read some of the interview questions.)

You will want to use these questions and even come up with your own. You will have five minutes to interview your partner. You will be told when the time is up and then your partner will ask you some questions. When you write down the three things you have in common with your partner, remember to think about what you learned in the interview.

Enrichment and Multicultural Activities

The following activities are designed to promote multicultural awareness, encourage cooperative learning, and incorporate the friendship-building process into an integrated learning curriculum.

These ideas can be used to enhance the lesson for the partners as well as the whole class. All the activities relate to the topic of the lesson.

1. Have the students research the meaning of and the origin of their names. By doing this activity they will find that their names might have originated from a particular culture, or be the result of generational trends. (e.g. in the 1980's many people were named Tiffany, Eric, Christopher).

2. Have a class discussion about physical appearances. Students should talk about which characteristics can be changed and which ones need to be accepted. Commonalities of race and sex can be discussed so the children will begin to understand that people shouldn't be labeled as looking one particular way because they are of a certain race or from a certain culture.

3. Have the students use crayons to trace around another student who is lying on a large sheet of paper or have them use chalk on the playground blacktop. Be sure to ask the children to use chalk or crayons that match the students' skin tones.

4. Make a list of the body parts on an outline of the human body. The class can label each part with words used in other languages.

5. Teach the children to say "hello" in other languages.

6. Partners can make paper dolls with hair and clothes that look like each other.

7. During PE, students can play "Simon Says" and use their partner to obey the game commands such as "Simon says, touch your partner's nose."

8. Play a game in which a chosen student has to find all of the class members who have red hair or blue eyes, or all of the students who are taller than four feet. This game will help students become more aware of similarities.

9. Have students play a game where they shake hands, elbows, feet, and other body parts with everyone in the class. Letting students act a little bit silly will help them get to know each other without embarassment.

10. Take a camera head shot of each student in class. Let the children

make jigsaw puzzles by cutting the photographs into pieces. Have other students put the puzzles together.

Suggested Children's Literature

The following list of children's books will enhance the focus of this lesson and help students examine the feelings and challenges that other young people face.

Grades K - 3

- *Arnie and the New Kid* by Nancy Carlson. Viking, 1990.

- *Andy (That's My Name)* by Tomie DePaola. Prentice Hall, 1973.

- *Why Am I Different?* by Nora Simon. Albert Whitman & Company, 1976.

- *People* by Peter Spier. Doubleday, 1980.

- *Benjie* by Joan M. Lexau. Dial Press, 1964.

- *Titch* by Pat Hutchins. Delacorte, 1975.

Grades 4 - 6

- *Turtle Knows Your Name* by Bryan Ashley. Atheneum, 1989.

- *Blubber* by Judy Blume. Bradbury, 1974.

- *Last Names First . . . And Some First Names Too* by Mary Price Lee and Richard S. Lee. Westminister Press, 1985.

- *A Blue Eyed Daisy* by Cynthia Ryland. Bradbury, 1985.

- *Deenie* by Judy Blume. Bradbury, 1973.

Getting to Know My Partner

Lesson 1
Interview

1. What is your full name?

____

2. How tall are you? Feet ______ Inches ______

3. What color are your eyes?

   Blue ______ Green ______ Brown ______ Other ______

4. Do you have a nickname? Yes ______ No ______ If so, what is it?

5. Do you have a favorite name that you would like to be called?

6. Do you have a birthmark? Yes ______ No ______

7. Do you wear glasses? Yes ______ No ______

8. Do you wear sunglasses? Yes ______ No ______

9. What size shoe do you wear? ______

10. What color clothes do you like to wear?

11. Do you ever blush? Yes ______ No ______

Here are three things we have in common.

____

____

____

Getting to Know My Partner

Lesson 1
Art

Materials Needed: crayons or marking pens, scissors, glue, pencil.

Directions:
1. Look at your partner's face and find out what color his or her eyes are. How is his or her mouth shaped? What shape are the eyes? What color and length of hair does he or she have? Does your partner have freckles, braces, or dimples?

2. Find a mouth, a nose, and a set of eyes on this page that looks like your partner's. Cut them out and glue them inside the face on the artwork page.

3. Color the face to match your partner's skin, eyes, and mouth. Draw some hair. Put some clothes on the figure and color the clothes to match your partner's.

Getting to Know My Partner

Lesson 1
Art

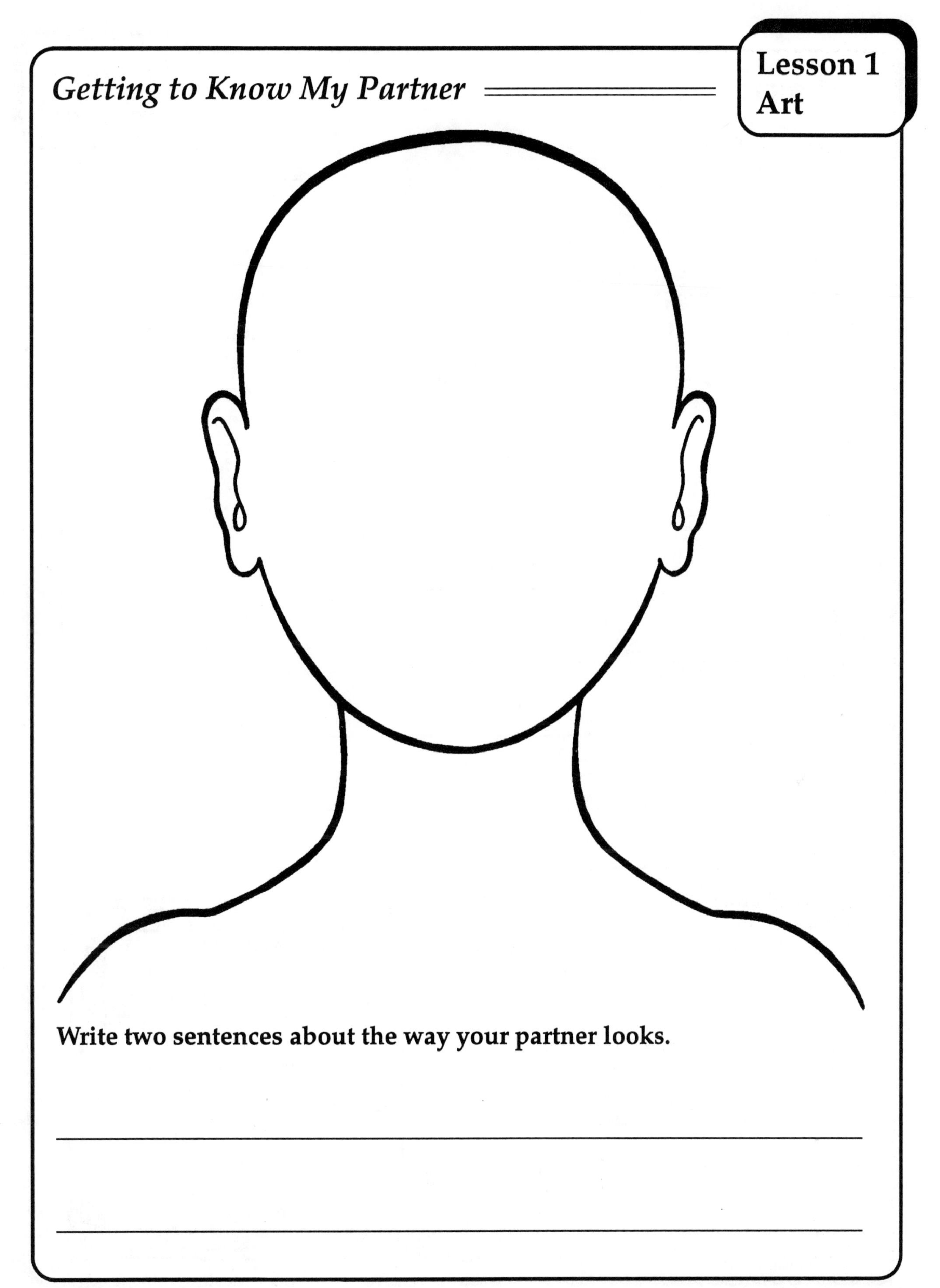

Write two sentences about the way your partner looks.

____

____

Getting to Know My Partner

Lesson 1 Writing

Handshake
They reach
Hands touch
Warm
Friendly
Bonding differences.
Erica Phillips
San Diego, California

Read each poem. Then write a poem about how your partner looks.

Sisters and Brothers
Norman has glasses and a round smiling face,
Sally has brown pigtails and a collar with lace,
Bobbie and Marshall have each lost teeth
And the boy who's eating Fritos is Keith.

Tommy and Rhonda have black skin,
Jason and Jeff are very, very thin,
Lori and Manny have blonde hair
Diane has green beads to wear.

Though none are exactly like the other,
All of them are sisters and brothers.

Jane Brucker
LaMesa, California

Appearances Aren't the Same
Appearances aren't the same
They're like a game.

You go to different places,
And always meet new faces.

Some are happy, some are sad,
And some even look real mad.

Charles Fox
St. Petersburg, Florida

Lesson 2: My Partner's Family

Overview and Objectives

During the early stages of this friendship-building program, the main objective is to help students find things in their lives they have in common. This helps the children relate to each other more easily outside the interview setting and soon begin a bonding relationship.

In establishing a friendship, it is important to deal with factual experiences first, as this lesson does, and then later talk about interests and feelings. When two people meet, it is quite common for them to want to find out about each other by exchanging simple information about their backgrounds. Family and home are topics every student is well acquainted with and Lesson 2 is designed to encourage discovery in this area.

The interview questions help the students find out positive facts about their partners' family members and home life. Often children consider their pets a very important part of the family, so questions have been included about animal family members, as well. The artwork activity allows the children to complete a family picture gallery, and the writing activity provides an opportunity for creative expression on the subject of unusual pets.

Getting Started

Read the interview questions aloud to your students. The following discussion questions can help set the stage for the weekly topic.

- Where are the different kinds of places a person can live? (Discuss both urban and rural settings.)

- What are the different kinds of homes people live in? (Discuss a variety of types of homes such as houses, apartments, condominiums, trailers.)

- Can you name some of the words that are used for relatives? (aunt, uncle, cousin, stepparent, etc.)

- What kind of pets do children have and what names are they given?

Lesson Format

Let the students know that the purpose of the art activity is to create a family picture gallery. Explain to the class that the information discovered through the interview will help with the art activity. Have the students interview each other. The interviews should only take about five to ten minutes per student.

The students will make pipe cleaner figures to represent the members of their partners' family and glue them inside the frames on the artwork page. If the partners' families are small, they can also include a family pet and/or extended family members to fill in the frames. You might make a simple diagram on the board to show how a fish, dog, cat, or lizard could be created from pipe cleaners.

If a student's family has more members than is provided for on the artwork page, then an extra sheet can be provided or the child should be allowed to have just five members put in the gallery with the names of the others listed on the page.

You may want the children to write the names of the family members (or pets) under the gallery frames. The words should be written neatly and in small print. If you decide to do this, the students will need to bring a list of their family members' names to class before the art activity begins.

Show your students an example of the artwork they will be doing for their Partner Books. Explain what a picture gallery is. The artwork directions should be read aloud to younger students to be sure they understand the steps. Make sure all the necessary materials are available.

Suggestions:
The pipe cleaners should be cut into pieces ahead of time. Yarn or toothpicks also could be used, if more appropriate for the class.

Have the students practice making one character while you watch. Check to be sure they are following the directions. Remind the students to write two *positive* sentences at the bottom of the artwork page about their partner's family. Allow the glue to dry overnight before putting the pages in the Partner Books.

The writing page includes poems written by other students. Ask the children to read the poems aloud to each other and then write a description of an unusual pet they could give to their partner.

Enrichment and Multicultural Activities

The following activities are designed to promote multicultural awareness, encourage cooperative learning, and incorporate the friendship-building process into an integrated learning curriculum.

These ideas can be used to enhance the lesson for the partners as well as the whole class. All the activities relate to the topic of the lesson.

1. Use a world map to locate where your students' families came from.

2. Invite speakers to talk to the class about the countries from which the students' families came. Parents can be a good resource for this activity.

3. Allow students who are from other countries to talk about their customs and beliefs.

4. Draw a timeline which lists the years the students were born and shows important times in their lives. Point out how events in the students' lives overlap.

5. Discuss one of the following topics:

- What is the purpose of a name?
- Who decides on a person's name?
- Where do names originate?
- What would it be like to be an orphan?
- How would it feel to be adopted?

6. Make a graph showing the number of people in your students' families.

7. Have each child bring in a photograph of his or her family. Read the poem "Something for Everyone" from the book *Free to be a Family* by Marlo Thomas. Encourage the students to share their photos and introduce the people in their pictures to the rest of the class.

8. Ask the students to invite their parents to an afternoon tea which the children prepare. Let the students welcome and serve their partner's parents, instead of their own parents.

9. Invite the brothers and sisters of your students to visit the class. The students can put on a play or a puppet show to entertain the visitors.

10. The names of your students can be used as spelling words until everyone can spell the names of the whole class.

Suggested Children's Literature

The following list of children's books will enhance the focus of this lesson and help students examine the feelings and challenges that other young people face.

Grades K - 3

- *Why Couldn't I Be An Only Kid Like You, Wigger?* by Barbara S. Hazen. Atheneum, 1975.

- *The Brute Family* by Russell Hoban. Macmillan, 1976.

- *All Kinds of Families* by Norma Simon. Albert Whitman, 1975.

- *The Keeping Quilt* by Patricia Polacco. Simon & Schuster, 1988.

- *Black Is Brown Is Tan* by Arnold Adoff. Harper & Row, 1973.

- *The Perfect Family* by Nancy Carlson. Puffin, 1985.

- *How My Family Lives in America* by Susan Kuklin. Bradbury (MacMillan Children's Book Division), 1992.

Grades 4 - 6

- *Got Me a Story to Tell* by Sylvia Yee and Lisa Kokin. St. John's Educational Threshold Center, 1977.

- *Where In the World Is the Perfect Family?* by Amy Hest. Clarion Books, 1989.

- *Families: A Celebration of Diversity, Commitment, and Love* by Aylette Jenness. Houghton Mifflin, 1990.

- *Like Jake and Me* by Mavis Jukes. Knopf, 1984.

- *Roses Sing on New Snow* by Paul Yee. MacMillan, 1990.

- *Koya Delaney & the Good Girl Blues* Eloise Greenfield. Scholastic, 1992.

- *Now Is Your Time! The African-American Struggle for Freedom* by Walter Deal Myers. Harper Collins, 1992.

- *Somewhere in the Darkness* by Walter Dean Myers. Scholastic, 1992.

My Partner's Family

Lesson 2 Interview

1. Who lives with you at home?

2. Where do you and your family live? House _______ Apartment _______

   Condominium _______ Trailer _______ Other _______

3. How many brothers do you have? _______ How old are they? _______

4. How many sisters do you have? _______ How old are they? _______

5. Do your grandparents live in your city? Yes _______ No _______

   If not, where do they live?

6. Do you have any cousins? Yes _______ No _______

   Do you have any aunts? Yes _______ No _______

   Do you have any uncles? Yes _______ No _______

   Do any of them live near you? Yes _______ No _______

7. Do you have a pet? What kind is it?

8. What is your pet's name? ______________________________

9. What kind of pet would you like to have? ______________________________

Here are three things both our families have in common.

____

____

____

My Partner's Family

Lesson 2
Art

Materials Needed: 3 short pipe cleaner pieces per person in your partner's immediate family, crayons, magic markers or colored pens, yarn, felt scraps, tissue paper scraps, glue, pencil.

Directions:

1. Find out how many people are in your partner's immediate family. Who are they? What are their names?

2. Use three pipe cleaner pieces for each family member.

3. Place pipe cleaners on the artwork page in the picture frames as follows:

   Step 1 - Place pipe cleaner pointing down. This is the body.
   Step 2 - Cross the second pipe cleaner over the first to make the arms of the person.
   Step 3 - Place the last piece at the bottom of the cross so that it forms an upside-down V. These are the legs.

4. Glue the pipe cleaners on your paper. Put glue on each pipe cleaner, not on the paper. Make a body for each family member.

5. Let the pipe cleaners dry before going on to the next step.

6. After the pipe cleaners have dried, draw heads on top of the bodies. Draw in eyes, hair, and clothes to match what your partner's family would look like.

7. Color the hair and clothes with crayons. Ask your partner which colors are correct. You may use yarn, felt, or tissue paper scraps to decorate.

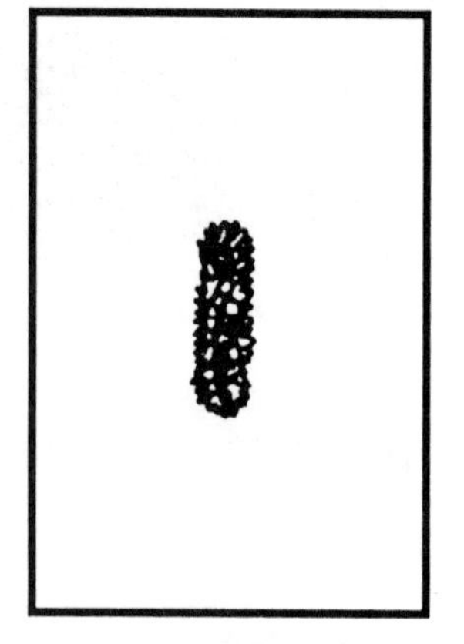
Step 1

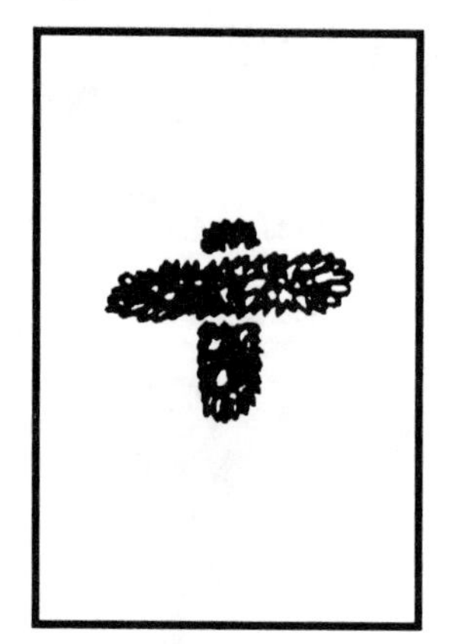
Step 2

Step 3

Finished Art

My Partner's Family
Lesson 2
Art
Here are two things I learned about my partner's family.

My Partner's Family

Read each poem. Then describe an unusual pet you could give to your partner.

Families
Houses are nice.
We live in them.
We live in families, too.
If we did not live in families,
We would each have to live in one house.
Then there would be billions of houses.
And if a person did not like his house,
He would have to move
into someone else's house.
So that's why we live in families.

Yael Falicov
San Diego, California

The Puppy
If I were a puppy,
I would always be sweet,
I would chase kittens
and their hearts would go
beat, beat.

If my master calls me,
I would go ahead,
because I don't want to be
the puppy that would not
be fed.
I like my master and
my master likes me.
I want to give him a good life

so it would just be
him and me.

Lorenzo Rosas
San Diego, California

Lesson 3: What My Partner Does at Home

Overview and Objectives

There are certain activities that almost all children do in their free time, regardless of their age or sex. Riding bikes, watching TV, and playing with neighbors and friends are as natural as eating ice cream and chewing gum. In addition to having certain games and hobby interests in common, most children will have similar household chores to do such as: washing dishes, taking out the garbage, and cleaning bedrooms.

Lesson 3 stresses the similarities of your students' home activities, and at the same time gives them a chance to talk about what goes on in their lives outside the classroom. It is important to broaden the base for friendship. Once the partners discover shared tasks and activities, they may get together outside of school, especially if they live in the same vicinity.

Getting Started

Discuss the lesson topic and try to get the children excited about finding out what their partner does after school and on weekends. A good discussion question might be, "What do you do in your free time?"

Read the interview questions aloud to your students. Remind the students to think of three things they have in common with their partners about what they do at home.

Explain that the art activity asks the children to dress the body figure on the artwork page, using tissue paper. The tissue paper should match the partner's clothing. To do this, the students will have to carefully observe their partners. This repeated experience (see Lesson 1) should help the children become more relaxed with each other.

Go over the directions for completing the artwork page. Have the class read the chalkboard words on the direction page. Suggest to the children that they refer to these words for the correct spelling of activities their partners do when they complete the two sentences at the bottom of the artwork page.

Lesson Format

Have the students interview each other. The interviews should only take about five to ten minutes.

When the students create clothing for their partners from tissue paper, tell them there are two ways to use the paper to dress the figures. Either method produces an attractive picture without requiring artistic perfection from the student.

- Make tissue paper balls to glue onto the figure by tearing small pieces of paper and using pencil tips to roll the paper into individual balls. (This method adds a three-dimensional effect to the artwork and is a good eye/hand/muscle coordination exercise as well.)
- Tear the paper apart and glue flat pieces onto the figure.

Suggestion:
Do not give your students large pieces of tissue paper. Divide up the tissue among partner pairs and provide smaller pieces of paper to prevent waste.

A black thin-line marker can be used to outline details such as buttons, collars, and belts.

Have your students draw their partners doing one of the activities discussed during the interview. The illustration should go in the thought bubble. For example the child may be shown riding a skateboard or playing soccer. Allow the glue to dry before allowing the students to put their artwork pages in the Partner Books.

The writing page includes poems written by other students. Ask the children to read the poems aloud to each other and then write a riddle about a TV show their partners like.

Enrichment and Multicultural Activities

The following activities are designed to promote multicultural awareness, encourage cooperative learning, and incorporate the friendship-building process into an integrated learning curriculum.

These ideas can be used to enhance the lesson for the partners as well as the whole class. All the activities relate to the topic of the lesson.

1. Ask students to find out what children in other countries might do to help out around their homes. Is it the same or different than what is

done in the United States?

2. Have students name and/or draw some of the places that people around the world call their home: apartments, cars, tepees, huts, igloos, condominiums, boats, tents, houses, garages, etc.

3. Bring in three to four games that children in other countries play. Show the students how to play these games.

4. Ask students to discuss what it would feel like to be a child: on an island, in the mountains, near the beach, in the city, in the country.

5. Brainstorm answers to the following questions which represent reality for most children around the world:

- How would you cook without a gas or electric stove?
- What could you do for fun if you had no television?
- What would you eat if you didn't have a grocery store nearby?

6. Make a class map which shows where all of the children live in the neighborhood. Designate the students' homes with flags or pins. Have the students find who lives close to them. This activity can double as a geography lesson.

7. The children can take a class poll about the following activities:

- Who watches TV cartoons on Saturdays?
- Who rides a bicycle to school?
- Who rides bicycles after school?
- When do the students do their homework?
- What are the most common household chores?

8. Divide the class into groups and ask the students to make a list of the specific steps necessary to do a household job such as making a bed, changing a bicycle tire, or setting the table. Be sure to include both partners in the groups. Afterwards, have the children trade lists to find out if, by reading their new lists, they can perform the task another group wrote about.

9. Have the children talk about all of the things they can do by themselves, without any help from others. This can lead to a class discussion about home activities which the students have in common.

10. Ask students to bring one item from home that tells something special about their family.

Suggested Children's Literature

The following list of children's books will enhance the focus of this lesson and help students examine the feelings and challenges that other young people face.

Grades K - 3

- *Bullfrog Builds a House* by Rosamond Dauer. Greenwillow, 1977.
- *My Friend William Moved Away* by March Whitmore Hickman. Abingdon, 1979.
- *You Ought to See Herbert's House* by Doris Lund. Watts, 1973.
- *How a House is Built* by Gail Gibbons. Holiday House, 1990.
- *Treasure Nap* by Juanita Havill. Houghton Mifflin, 1992.
- *How We Live* by Anita Harper. Harper & Row, 1977.
- *Loudmouth George and the New Neighbors* by Nancy Carlson. Puffin, 1986.
- *Henry and Mudge and the Long Weekend* by Cynthia Ryland. Bradbury Press, 1972.

Grades 4 - 6

- *Homes in Cold Places* by Alan James. Lerner Publications, 1989.
- *People of the Breaking Day* by Marcia Sewell. Atheneum, 1990.
- *Somebody Else's Child* by Roberta Silman. Frederick Warne, 1976.

What My Partner Does at Home

Lesson 3
Interview

1. What do you usually do at home after school?

2. What do you do on weekends?

3. What things do you do to help around the house?

4. What jobs do you do to get spending money?

5. How do you use your spending money?

6. What is the best thing you have bought with money you have earned?

7. What are some of the things you do with your friends after school?

8. Do you watch TV cartoons on Saturdays and Sundays?

9. When do you do your homework?

10. Do you live near any of your classmates? Do you ever play with anyone in your class after school?

11. What time do you go to bed?

Here are three things we have in common about things we do at home.

____

____

____

What My Partner Does at Home

Lesson 3
Art

Materials Needed: tissue paper strips or scraps, glue sticks, black thin-line marker, pencil.

Directions:

1. Look at your partner. What is he or she wearing? What are the colors in his or her clothes? What color hair does your partner have?

2. Get tissue paper that matches the colors you see.

3. Tear the tissue paper into small pieces.

4. Arrange the tissue paper inside the figure on the artwork page. The colors should match how your partner looks.

5. Glue the tissue paper on the page. Use the glue very carefully. Do not put too much glue on the paper.

6. Use a thin-line black marker to draw in eyes and mouth on the face. Use the marker to draw in parts of clothing such as belts, buttons, and collars.

7. Draw one activity in the thought bubble that your partner does at home. The activity should be something you found out about your partner during the interview.

8. Try to draw an activity that both you and your partner like to do.

What My Partner Does at Home

Lesson 3
Art

Write two sentences about what your partner does at home. Use your partner's first name in each sentence.

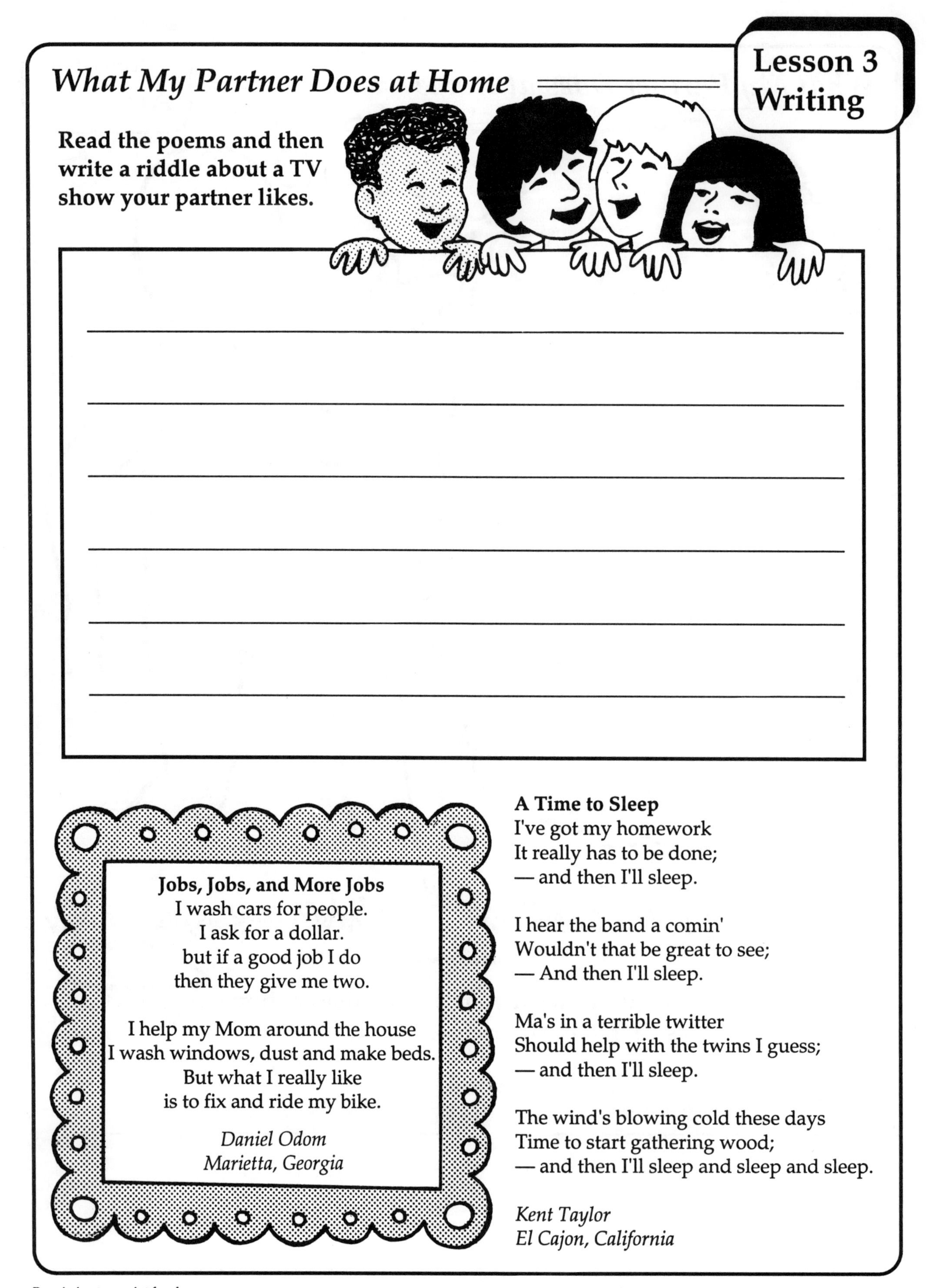

What My Partner Does at Home

Lesson 3 Writing

Read the poems and then write a riddle about a TV show your partner likes.

Jobs, Jobs, and More Jobs
I wash cars for people.
I ask for a dollar.
but if a good job I do
then they give me two.

I help my Mom around the house
I wash windows, dust and make beds.
But what I really like
is to fix and ride my bike.

Daniel Odom
Marietta, Georgia

A Time to Sleep
I've got my homework
It really has to be done;
— and then I'll sleep.

I hear the band a comin'
Wouldn't that be great to see;
— And then I'll sleep.

Ma's in a terrible twitter
Should help with the twins I guess;
— and then I'll sleep.

The wind's blowing cold these days
Time to start gathering wood;
— and then I'll sleep and sleep and sleep.

Kent Taylor
El Cajon, California

Lesson 4: My Partner's Favorite Things

Overview and Objectives

Elementary school students quickly develop opinions about what they like best. It is not unusual for them to have definite favorites in almost every category. For example, children will tell you, in no uncertain terms, what are their favorite ice cream flavors, television shows, colors, movies, and recess games.

By the time they reach the fourth grade, students are no longer satisfied with whatever is presented to them— they want choices. Increasingly, their choices are influenced by their friends and the most current fads. Whatever is "in" becomes what everyone wants.

This hypothesis was tested during an Interest Survey completed by about two hundred fourth, fifth, and sixth-graders. The results show that no matter who the children were or what their special problems, they all had the same favorites in several areas.

- Almost all the children love to eat hamburgers and drink soft drinks.
- The most popular TV shows were listed as their favorites.
- Most of them enjoyed the common games which were played at their schools during recess.

Children at this age make the same choices because they want to be accepted. Lesson 4 focuses on helping students discover what things are everyone's favorites.

Getting Started

Before the interview, art, and writing sessions begin, have your students cut out an assortment of pictures and words relating to these categories:

- cars
- toys and games
- food

- sports equipment
- people playing different sports
- clothes for both boys and girls
- colors
- animals

You can find these pictures and words in the following types of publications:

- newspaper ads
- sports magazines
- fashion magazines
- home and garden magazines
- newspaper magazines
- department store catalogs
- used greeting cards

Store the cutout pictures and words in a file box by categories. Large labeled envelopes work well. Set up the categories ahead of time so the students will know where to file their cutouts. You may want to make a word and picture collage of your own to show the children what the finished project should look like and to motivate them to do the same thing. In addition to identifying their own interests, the children will also develop skills in fine motor coordination, eye-hand coordination, sorting, classification, and evaluation.

Lesson Format

Explain to the children that they will be making a montage of some of their partners' favorite things. To do this, they will need to complete the interview to find out more about their partners. Go over the interview questions and artwork directions with your students.

Ask the students to interview each other. The interviews should take about five to ten minutes. Remind the children to write two sentences at the bottom of the artwork page about their partners' favorite things. They must use their partners' first name in each sentence. After the montages are completed, allow the artwork to dry before placing the pages in the Partner Books.

The writing page includes poems written by other students. Ask the children to read the poems aloud to each other and then make up a song about favorite things. You might want to have the children listen to the song about favorite things from the movie *The Sound of Music*. Play the music and stop after the words "These are a few of my favorite things . . . ." Have the children name *their* favorite things.

Enrichment and Multicultural Activities

The following whole class activities are designed to promote multicultural awareness, encourage cooperative learning, and incorporate the friendship-building process into an integrated learning curriculum.

These ideas can be used to enhance the lesson for the partners as well as the whole class. All the activities relate to the topic of the lesson.

1. Bring in educational and geographical magazines and ask students to try to find examples of clothing people in other countries wear. Ask these questions:

- In what ways is the clothing similar to what is worn in the United States? In what ways is their dress different?

- Do you see any outfits that our fashions might have copied?

2. Have students pick three to five places that are geographically close to the United States (e.g. Canada, Mexico, Central America, the Bahamas.) Have them work in teams and research with encyclopedias to find out what children like to do in these countries. They could answer the questions:

- What games do they play?

- What foods do they eat?

3. For homework, ask the students to write down the names of as many restaurants in their town, city, or area as they can. Have the students answer these questions:

- What kind of food do these restaurants serve?

- What is their favorite dish and why?

4. Make a list of every kind of car students can name. Add a few of your own. Then ask the children to find out where they are built. Use a map to point out the places.

5. Have students interview students from the ESL and/or special education classes in their school to see what they have in common.

6. Go to the ice cream store and buy three to five quarts of unusual flavors. Be sure to get plastic spoons and cups so the students can sample from each flavor. Have the children rate the flavors according to their favorite taste.

7. Have the children conduct a class poll of favorites and make a mural of the most highly-rated items.

8. Discuss with the class why certain things are popular. Talk about how much their friends' opinions

influence them.

9. Ask the students to make lists of what each classmate does best. You can make certificates for the class and fill in the skills in which each child is most proficient.

10. Have the students bring in an item or picture that reminds them of a favorite place, cherished possession, or pleasant memory.

Suggested Children's Literature

The following list of children's books will enhance the focus of this lesson and help students examine the feelings and challenges that other young people face.

Grades K - 3

- *Maude and Sally* by Nicki Weiss. Greenwillow, 1983.

- *Bread, Bread, Bread* by Ann Morris. Lothrop, Lee & Shepard Books, 1989.

- *Where Do You Go to School?* by Caroline Arnold. Watts, 1982.

- *Rosa & Marco and the Three Wishes* by Barbara Brenner. Bradbury, 1992.

- *Walter's Tail* by Lisa Campbell Ernst. Bradbury, 1992.

Grades 4 - 6

- *Guess Who My Favorite Person Is?* by Byrd Baylor. Macmillan, 1985.

- *Stuffer* by Peter Parnall. Macmillan 1992.

- *Dragon Magic* by Andre Norton. Thomas Y. Crowell, 1972.

My Partner's Favorite Things

Lesson 4
Interview

1. What kind of ice cream do you like best?
2. What are some of your favorite foods?
3. What toy do you like best?
4. What game do you like best?
5. What sports do you like to play? Why?
6. What kind of clothes do you like to wear most of the time?
7. What is your favorite color?
8. What is your favorite kind of car?
9. What animal do you like best?
10. What is your favorite candy?
11. Do you have a day of the week you like best? Why?

Here are three things we have in common
on our list of favorite things.

____

____

____

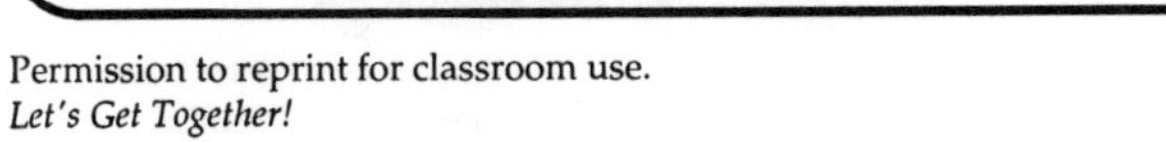

My Partner's Favorite Things

Lesson 4
Art

Materials Needed: pre-cut magazine and newspaper pictures and words, small flashcards to use to make words not cut out of magazines, scissors, glue, pencil.

Directions:

1. Think about all the things that your partner said he or she likes.

2. Go through the picture collection and pick out at least six things that your partner likes. Try to find things you both like.

3. Go through the word cut-outs and try to find words that describe the pictures you picked. If you can't find a word, take a flashcard and write a word on it that describes the picture.

4. Arrange pictures and words on the artwork page in your own design. Look at the example done by your teacher.

5. Glue your pictures on the paper and put the words over, under, or on the pictures in your own design.

My Partner's Favorite Things

Lesson 4
Art

Write two sentences about your partner's favorite things.
Use your partner's first name in each sentence.

My Partner's Favorite Things

Lesson 4
Writing

Read each poem. Then make up a song about some favorite things.

____

____

____

____

____

____

Sixth-Grade Camp
"It's dark."
"I know. Stay together."
"Hey, follow me."
"Get off my foot!"
"Are you trying to hold my hand?"
"I want to go back. I don't like it here."
"I think I have poison ivy."
"Did you hear that?"
"What?"
"It sounded like a wolf."
"Naw, the wolf's over here. Is there
a full moon out tonight, or what?"
"I thought I heard a rattlesnake."
"That's it - I'm leaving!"
"I think we're lost."
"I have to use the bathroom."
"I'm sleepy. They get us up too early."
"I think I see a light."
"Where's the North Star?"
"What are you, an astrologer or something?"
"I think we're heading toward New Jersey."
"I love sixth-grade camp."
"Let's do this again next year."
"Don't worry, you probably will."

Monica Pearson
San Diego, California

My Favorite Things
A blue dress with a red collar,
A humpty-dumpty glass that holds my water,
My mom and dad, and our dog Rusty,
The dollhouse my brother built,
(Even though it's a little dusty),
Tulips, school, and almond-chocolate bars,
Birthdays, Christmas, and rides in sportcars —
These are a few of my favorite things,
Because JOY and HAPPINESS all of these bring.

Jane Brucker
La Mesa, California

Lesson 5: My Partner at School

Overview and Objectives

Being in the same classroom gives students a common bond. Unfortunately, it does not always guarantee that they will be friends or even interact socially. Research shows that proximity is not enough. Even when the teacher assigns a group project, the students will not automatically accept each other. They will often be more involved in completing the task than getting to know one another.

Lesson 5 is designed to help your students discuss school activities with which they are both familiar. All youngsters like and dislike something about school. Since the children often share many of the same ideas and feelings about school, this discussion should widen the roads of communication between them as they learn more about each other.

Lesson Format

Go over the interview questions and the artwork directions with your students. Make sure all the materials for the art activity are available to the students.

It would be helpful to show your students an example of the finished art project. Since the students will be using cutout pictures to represent their partner involved in a school activity, ask a few of the children to draw details on the person sitting at the desk in your sample, to look like you. Explain to the students that they will have to add details to the person sitting at the desk on their page, so he or she will look like their partner.

Write the following sentences on the chalkboard. Use manuscript writing if appropriate.

___________ is in the ______ grade.

___________ likes ___________
in school.

Have your student copy these sentences at the bottom of the artwork page and fill in the correct information. Remind the class to allow the glue to dry on the artwork pages before they are placed in the Partner Books.

The writing page includes poems written by other students. Ask the children to read the poems aloud to each other and then write a poem about school for their partner. The poems could begin with the things their partners like least and conclude with the things that are liked best.

Poem Pattern:

1 word	Math
2 words	Science, History
3 words	Recess, Art, Music
2 words	Lunch, PE
1 word	Reading

Enrichment and Multicultural Activities

The following activities are designed to promote multicultural awareness, encourage cooperative learning, and incorporate the friendship-building process into an integrated learning curriculum.

These ideas can be used to enhance the lesson for the partners as well as the whole class. All the activities relate to the topic of the lesson.

1. Have the student who is not socially accepted or has a learning disability, tutor another child in something that he or she knows or does really well. Every student will have at least a few good skills.

2. Teach the class how to say "school" in various languages.

3. For homework, have students interview their parents or grandparents to find out who their favorite teacher was and why. Also find out where they were educated. Did their parents go to schools in different states or countries?

4. Ask the children to pick a story that deals with students from other countries.

5. Have students use encyclopedias to find out what education is like both in various countries and in other times.

6. Let the students take turns being the teacher for a period of time each day or once a week. Give each child a turn. The student who is playing teacher should think of one thing he or she does well, and then teach it to the rest of the class. Examples are: cooking a special dish, playing a new game, spelling words, using a certain tool, crocheting, drawing, etc.

7. Conduct a class discussion using one of these open-ended sentences:

- My classmates think I am _______.

- School is ____________________.

- At school I am _________________.

- The things I like best about my classmates are _________________.

- I'd like school better if _________.

8. Divide the students into small groups and have them write five class rules that would help everyone get along. *The reproducible worksheet on page 64 can be used for this activity.*

Tell the children to write the rules in a positive manner such as: "Get permission to speak," instead of: "Don't talk out in class." Have each group choose a representative for a class council which will then select the five best rules.

9. Using the information from the interview questions in Lessons 1 through 4, play a guessing game about someone in the class. List the things a certain person likes to do and see who can guess the name of the student first.

10. Make a TODAY IS ________'S DAY bulletin board. The partner and the honored student can design the bulletin board together. Make sure every student has an opportunity to be honored. More than one student can be honored at a time (e.g. maybe both partners or two sets of partners).

Suggested Children's Literature

The following list of children's books will enhance the focus of this lesson and help students examine the feelings and challenges that other young people face.

Grades K - 3

- *First Grade Can Wait* by Lorraine Aseltine. Albert Whitman, 1988.

- *Angel Child, Dragon Child* by Michele Surat. Scholastic, 1989.

- *Will I Have a Friend?* by Miriam Cohen. Macmillan, 1967.

- *The Best Bug to Be* by Dolores Johnson. MacMillan, 1992.

- *School Fair* by Althea. Cambridge University Press, 1983.

- *School Days* by B. G. Hennessy. Viking Child Books, 1990.

- *School Friends* by Bernice Chardiet and Grace Maccorone. Scholastic, Inc. 1991.

Grades 4 - 6

- *Victor* by Claire Galbraith. Little, 1971.

- *The Hundred Dresses* by Eleanor Estes. Harcourt, 1944.

- *Crow Boy* by Taro Yashima. Viking, 1955.

CLASS RULES

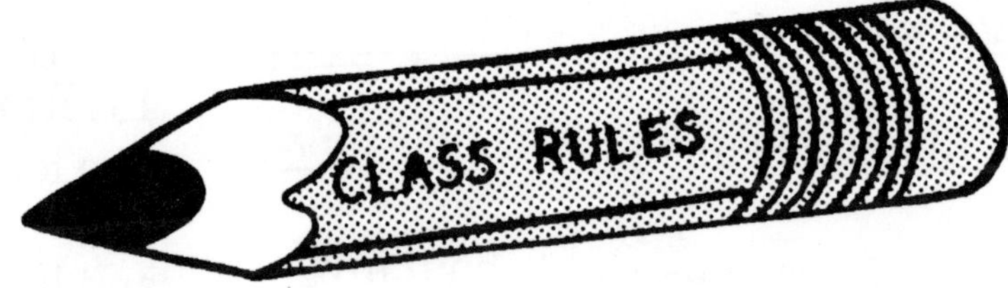

1. ______________________________

____

____

2. ______________________________

____

3. ______________________________

____

4. ______________________________

____

____

5. ______________________________

____

My Partner at School

Lesson 5
Interview

1. What grade do you like best? _______

2. What activity do you like best in school? Art _______ Science _______

   Math _______ Reading _______ Social Studies_______ Other _______

3. What activity do you not like in school? _______________________

4. What field trip would you like to go on? _______________________

5. What do you like best about recess time? _______________________

6. Who do you know in the school who is not in your classroom?

7. Do you have any brothers or sisters who go to the same school as you?

8. Do you like to work at your own desk or at a table with other classmates?

9. What do you like best to do in the classroom to help the teacher?

10. What is your favorite free time activity in class?

Here are three things we both like to do in school.

____

____

____

My Partner at School

Lesson 5
Art

Materials Needed: scissors, crayons or colored pencils, glue, pencil.

Directions:

1. Think about the things your partner likes to do at school.
2. Cut out three of the activities below that your partner likes to do.
3. Glue the pictures in the boxes on the artwork page.
4. Color in the page. Try to make the person on the page look like your partner.
5. Draw in details such as hair, and clothes your partner is wearing.
6. Fill in the blanks of these two sentences and copy them on your artwork page.

_________________ is in the _____________ grade.

_________________ likes _________________ in school.

My Partner at School
Lesson 5
Art
Copy the two sentences about your partner here.

My Partner at School

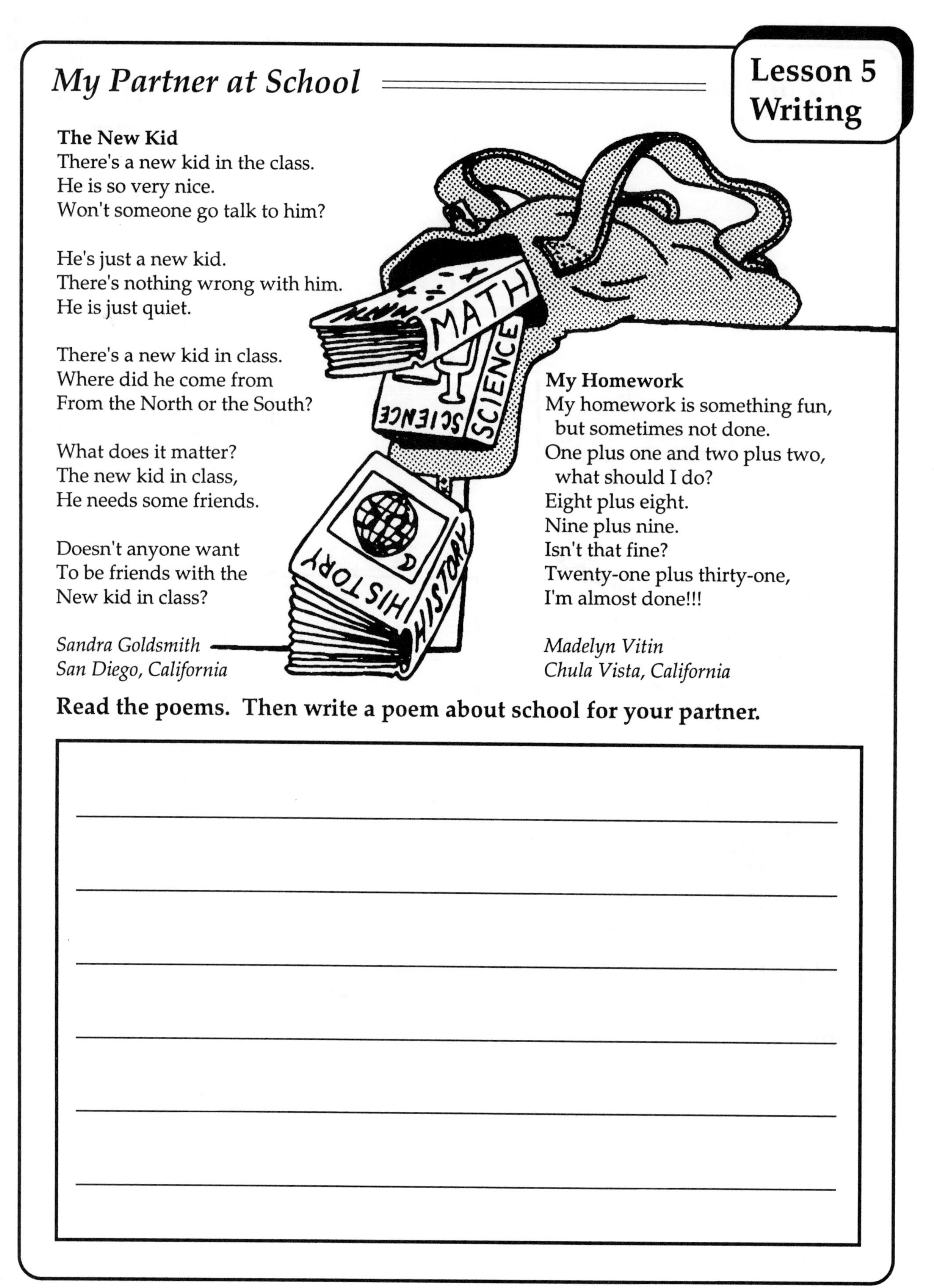

The New Kid
There's a new kid in the class.
He is so very nice.
Won't someone go talk to him?

He's just a new kid.
There's nothing wrong with him.
He is just quiet.

There's a new kid in class.
Where did he come from
From the North or the South?

What does it matter?
The new kid in class,
He needs some friends.

Doesn't anyone want
To be friends with the
New kid in class?

Sandra Goldsmith
San Diego, California

My Homework
My homework is something fun,
but sometimes not done.
One plus one and two plus two,
what should I do?
Eight plus eight.
Nine plus nine.
Isn't that fine?
Twenty-one plus thirty-one,
I'm almost done!!!

Madelyn Vitin
Chula Vista, California

Read the poems. Then write a poem about school for your partner.

Lesson 6: All About Entertainment

Overview and Objectives

So far this friendship-building program has been concerned with fact-finding discussions, covering broad areas. The students should be sufficiently comfortable with each other at this point to begin sharing their mutual interests in more specific categories.

Lesson 6 focuses on television and other types of entertainment that the students are interested in.

Lesson Format

Go over the interview questions and the artwork directions with your students. Make sure that each set of partners has a fairly recent copy of a TV guide from a Sunday newspaper. If possible, provide two used TV guides to each set of partners.

Ask the students to go through the guide together and pick out three to five shows that their partners like to watch. Then they should cut the listing out of the guide. If there are any special ads for the show, they can be cut out too. The cutouts will be glued inside the TV screen on the artwork page. Remind the students to write two sentences about some TV shows both partners like. The artwork pages should be allowed time to dry before they are placed in the Partner Books.

The writing page includes poems written by other students. Read the poems aloud to the students and then have them make up a "class" commercial to go with their favorite show.

Enrichment and Multicultural Activities

The following activities are designed to promote multicultural awareness, encourage cooperative learning, and incorporate the friendship-building process into an integrated learning curriculum.

These ideas can be used to enhance the lesson for the partners as well as the whole class. All the activities relate to the topic of the lesson.

1. Bring in an assortment of hats or pictures of hats representing different cultures (e.g. turban, fez, baseball cap, beret, cowboy hat, sombrero, tam-o-shanter, Indian headdress, derby, Chinese headdress, pioneer bonnet). Discuss the different people who might wear these.

2. Bring in several musical instruments or pictures of them. Talk about the instruments and their origins. Encourage students to bring in instruments they have at home and share them with the class.

3. Help the students learn some ethnic or folk dances. Allow volunteers from the class or from other classrooms to do the teaching, if they are familiar with a particular dance. Contact a local ethnic dance group and ask a representative to teach a dance to the children.

4. Play records or tapes of several different national anthems. Discuss the content of the lyrics and the importance of national pride.

5. Have students do research to find out about the current popular movie stars and singers in other countries. The children could report back to the class on the background of these famous personalities and which movies they were in or what songs they made popular. *The reproducible worksheet on page 72 can be used for this activity.*

6. Let the students role play a family watching TV. This can be a very humorous activity.

7. Make puppets and have a show, using different personalities from the class as models for the characters. Keep the show funny but positive. You can assign different students to play the same role. Do not let any of the students play themselves.

8. Take a poll in the class of favorite TV shows and movies. Bring in a movie critique to read to the children and then have the students write their own critiques of a movie they have seen. Encourage them to explain why they liked it or didn't like it. The reports can be shared with the class.

9. Play TV charades. Ask small groups to pantomime a TV show while the rest of the class guesses which program it is.

10. Encourage the students to put on a presentation to share interesting facts with their classmates from *Guinness World Book of Records* and/or *The Teacher's Book of Lists*. Their findings could make an interesting bulletin board.

Suggested Children's Literature

The following list of children's books will enhance the focus of this lesson and help students examine the feelings and challenges that other young people face.

Grades K - 3

- *Harlequin and the Gift of Many Colors* by Remy Charlip and Buston Supree. Parents Magazine, 1973.
- *Albert Goes Hollywood* by Henry Schwartz. Orchard Books, 1992.
- *Good Times on Grandfather Mountain* by Jacqueline Briggs Martin. Orchard Books, 1992.
- *Corgiville Fair* by Tasha Tudor. Harper Trophy, 1971.

Grades 4 - 6

- *Handtalk Zoo* by George and Mary Beth Ancona. Four Winds Press, 1989.
- *Oliver Button Is a Sissy* by Tomie DePaola. Harcourt, 1979.
- *Keep Laughing* by Cynthia D. Grant. Atheneum, 1991.
- *All of You Was Singing* by Richard Lewis. Atheneum, 1991.

Name ______________________________

FAMOUS STAR

Name of star ____

Country where star lives ______________________________________

Here are five facts I found out about this star:

1. ____

____

2. ____

____

3. ____

____

4. ____

____

5. ____

All About Entertainment

Lesson 6
Interview

1. Who or what do you like to watch best on TV?

2. What kind of movies do you like best? Comedy _______ Thriller_______

   Fantasy _______ Science Fiction _______ Western _______

   Animated _______ Other _______

3. What was the name of the last movie you saw?

4. What songs do you like best?

5. How many TVs do you have at home?

6. When do you watch TV?

7. What is your favorite TV show?

8. Which actor/actress do you like the most?

9. What is your favorite commercial?

10. What books do you like best?

11. Have you been to a play? What was it about?

Here are three TV shows or entertainers we both like.

____

____

____

All About Entertainment

Lesson 6
Art

Materials Needed: TV guides, glue, scissors, crayons, pencil.

Directions:

1. Think about the information you have learned as you were interviewing your partner. What were some of his or her favorite TV shows and movies?

2. Look through the TV guide with your partner, find three to five listings or special ads about shows he or she likes, and cut them out.

3. Glue them in the TV frame on the artwork page. Color the TV frame.

Write two sentences about TV shows you and your partner like.

All About Entertainment

Lesson 6 Writing

Read each poem. Then write a commercial to go with your partner's favorite show.

Commercials
Commercials, Commercials, we need you so.
If we didn't have you what would we know?

Commercials tell about the latest TV shows,
What's to come in the winter when it snows.

Commercials tell you about all the new things,
From potato chips to sparkling rings.

Commercials, Commercials, we need you so,
If we didn't have you what would we know?

Kevin Waters
Atlanta, Georgia

Circus Day 1980
"The Greatest Show On Earth"
With all of its stupendous array;
The Ringmaster's voice resounding
Throughout the arena today;
Seeing clever clowns, trained dogs, jungle cats,
Hearing the band and drum rolls for the bears
and other acts.
The wire-walkers,
bareback riders,
flying trapeze,
Ponderous Pachyderms perform with ease.

On the last day of the show
When the circus is packin' and leavin',
Only the memory of it all
Is what starts one a-grievin'.
The performance is ending
And the last chord is sounded,
Then the "Big Top's" suddenly empty . . .
Like a dream — confound it!

Lynne H. Beheim
San Diego, California

Lesson 7: All About Traveling

Overview and Objectives

Everyone enjoys talking about places they have traveled to, whether close to home or far away. It is twice as much fun when people discover that someone they know has visited a few of the same places.

Lesson 7 focuses on places the students have visited. The locations mentioned in the interview are the most common sites children might visit: zoo, amusement park, aquarium, camping site, relative's home.

As the children learn about the places their partners have visited, they will discover more about their commonalities.

Lesson Format

Go over the interview questions and discuss the specific tourist sites for your geographical area. Write the names of popular attractions on the chalkboard to help the students complete the questionnaire.

Have your students cut out pictures and words of different places to visit (zoo, museum, aquarium, amusement parks, beach, mountains, or desert) and modes of transportation (train, car, bus, airplane, camper, boat, bicycle, skates, skateboard).

These pictures and words can be found in magazines, newspaper ads, travel brochures, or store catalogs. The pictures should be only one or two inches big so they will fit into a traced footprint of the student.

Review the artwork directions with the class. It is recommend that poster board, or some other kind of thin cardboard be used for making the footprints. The students should leave their shoes on when tracing the footprints, and then make a pattern from the cardboard rather than tracing the shoe directly on the artwork page. The cardboard pattern is then used to trace onto the artwork page.

Remind the students to write two

sentences at the bottom of the artwork page — one which tells about where their partners would like to visit and one which tells about how their partners would like to travel. Allow the glue on the artwork pages to dry overnight before placing them in the Partner Books.

The writing page includes poems written by other students. Ask the children to read the poems aloud to each other and then write a riddle about a fun place to visit.

Enrichment and Multicultural Activities

The following activities are designed to promote multicultural awareness, encourage cooperative learning, and incorporate the friendship-building process into an integrated learning curriculum.

These ideas can be used to enhance the lesson for the partners as well as the whole class. All the activities relate to the topic of the lesson.

1. Create a time capsule called "Out of this World" whose purpose is to preserve only *one thing* from each of the main cultures in the United States: Blacks, Whites, Hispanics, Mexican Americans, Native Americans, Asian Americans.

2. Collect stamps from different countries and states. Have the children write letters to friends or relatives living in other places. A pen pal club could be started also.

3. Go to the local currency exchange and get samples of the currency of other lands. Ask students to bring in coins from different countries if they have them at home. Remind the children not to bring in currency that is valuable.

4. Teach about different time zones by making clocks to show times around the world. Use maps from airline magazines to incorporate into a math or social studies lesson.

5. Have the children figure the mileage from their city to places around world where their families originated.

6. Invite a travel agent to visit the classroom and bring brochures about the places from which the students or their families came.

7. Tell the students they are going on a trip to one of three very strange places: Planet of Darkness, Land of No Sound, or World on Wheels. Blindfold the children who are going to Planet of Darkness and assign each one a classmate who will take them on a predetermined path.

Use earmuffs or cotton for the students who are going to the Land of No Sound. The children who are going to World on Wheels will be assigned to wheelchairs. Later, have the students discuss how it felt to have that particular handicap. If appropriate, ask the students to write about these experiences.

8. For a Social Studies lesson, have the students look up their coat of arms or make banners symbolizing their name and/or where their family originated.

9. Arrange a field trip to: the airport, an art gallery, a factory, the planetarium, an electrical power plant.

10. Have the students make postcards about any place in the world they would like to visit. Make available: 5 x 9 index cards *(or see the reproducible worksheet on page 80)*, colorful pens, and maps, research books, atlases, encyclopedias, and travel brochures.

Each child decides on the place he or she wants to visit, draws a picture representative of that place on the front of the card, and writes a message on the back of the card about the imaginary trip. The messages should be addressed to other members of the class or to a partner.

Suggested Children's Literature

The following list of children's books will enhance the focus of this lesson and help students examine the feelings and challenges that other young people face.

Grades K - 3

- *George and Martha* by James Marshall. Houghton, 1972.
- *One to Teeter-Totter* by Edith Battles. Whitman, 1973.
- *I Do Not Like It When My Friend Comes to Visit* by Ivan Sherman. Harcourt, 1973.
- *Frog and Toad Together* by Arnold Lobel. Harper and Row, 1972.
- *The Weird Things in Nanna's House* by Ann Maree Mason. Orchard Books, 1992.
- *Hazel's Circle* by Sharon Phillips Denslowe. Four Winds Press, 1992.

Grades 4 - 6

- *The Bridge* by Emily Cheney Neville. Harper & Row, 1988.
- *City! New York* by Shirley Climo. MacMillan, 1990.
- *What the Dickens!* by Jane Louise Curry. MacMillan, 1991.

Dear ________________________,

To:

Dear ________________________,

To:

All About Traveling

Lesson 7 Interview

1. What cities have you been to?

2. What places have you visited? Zoo _______ Museum _______

   Aquarium _______ Amusement Park _______ Other _______

3. Do you ever go camping?

4. What place do you like to go to the most?

5. What is your favorite thing to do when you go to your favorite place?

6. How do you like to travel? Train _______ Car _______ Bus _______

   Airplane _______ Camper _______ Boat _______ Other _______

7. Who goes with you when you go on a trip?

8. Do you have any relatives who live in another city? Where do they live and who are they?

9. What time of the year do you usually go on a trip?

10. If you could go anywhere, where would you go? Why? Who would you take with you?

Here are three places we both have been to.

____

____

____

Lesson 7 Art

All About Traveling

Materials Needed: your partner's shoe, markers, cardboard, scissors, pictures and words of places to visit and ways to travel, extra flash-cards for writing names of places to visit and ways to travel, pencil.

Directions:

1. Trace your partner's shoe on a piece of cardboard. Cut the pattern out. It's OK for your partner to keep his or her shoes on.

2. Trace around the pattern on your artwork page, using a pencil. Turn the pattern diagonally so it will fit on the page. Try not to draw in the space where the sentences go. Trace over the outline with a marker.

3. Think about all the places your partner has visited.

4. Look through the pictures with your partner and find three to five pictures of places he or she has been to or would like to visit.

5. Look through the cutout words. Find some that tell where your partner has visited. If you need to, write some words on the blank flashcards.

6. Go through the transportation pictures and find one or two that show how your partner usually travels on trips or to school.

7. Glue your pictures and words on the shoeprint.

8. Color in the background. It can be grass, dirt, sand, cement, or asphalt.

All About Traveling

Lesson 7
Art

Write one sentence about where your partner would like to visit.
Write one sentence about how your partner would like to travel.

All About Traveling

Lesson 7 Writing

Trains
The train goes screaming in the dark,
The fiery light sends out a spark,
You hear the screeching of wheels from behind
Until it stops at the end of the line.

Todd Battenfield
La Mesa, California

Read the poems. Write a riddle about a fun place to visit. Let your partner try to guess the answer.

____

____

____

____

____

____

I Like to Visit Six Flags
I went to Six Flags Over Georgia this summer.
Without such a trip life would be a bummer.
I rode the "Scream Machine" two times.
For hours I had to stand in many lines.
It's a wild and scary roller coaster
That makes you feel like you're in a toaster.
Afterwards, I felt dizzy and turned
green like a lime,
But sure enough I had to do it
one more time.

Todd Greene
Smyrna, Georgia

Taking Off
The airplane taxis down the field
And heads into the breeze
It lifts its wheels above the ground,
It skims above the trees,
It rises high and higher
Away up toward the sun,
It's just a speck against the sky
— And now it's gone!

Unknown

Lesson 8: Hobbies My Partner Likes

Overview and Objectives

If a student cares enough about a certain interest to take it up as a hobby, he or she will probably be excited to talk about it. People always like to discuss their interests because it gives them an opportunity to feel like an expert.

Many of your students will have the same hobbies. After all, a hobby is nothing more than what a person does in his or her free time. The normal school day doesn't allow-students much time to discuss the things they enjoy as hobbies. Lesson 8 provides an opportunity for children to share these special interests.

This friendship-building lesson not only allows students to find out more about each other, but will also give you some new ideas for coordinating your classroom curriculum to specific student interests. Relating academic work to hobbies is a great way to get students excited about classwork.

Lesson Format

Let the students know that in this lesson they will be creating a coat of arms based on their partners hobbies and special interests. You may want to have the children research family coats of arms or historical banners to get acquainted with their original purpose.

Discuss the interview questionnaire and the artwork directions with the students. Make sure all the materials are available. Each student will need two pipe cleaners. If possible, present a sample of a finished art project showing the hobbies *you* enjoy.

Remind the students to write two sentences at the bottom of the artwork page telling about their partners' hobbies. Allow the glue on the artwork pages to dry overnight before placing them in the Partner Books.

The writing page includes poems written by other students. Ask the children to read the poems aloud to each other and then write a short story about their partners doing their favorite hobby.

Enrichment and Multicultural Activities

The following activities are designed to promote multicultural awareness, encourage cooperative learning, and incorporate the friendship-building process into an integrated learning curriculum.

These ideas can be used to enhance the lesson for the partners as well as the whole class. All the activities relate to the topic of the lesson.

1. Draw or color flags representing the countries of each student's origin. There are coloring books available with international flags.

2. Put students with the same hobby in a group and have them make a display for an old-fashioned fair. Your class may even invite other students from the rest of the school to come and visit. If some of your students have hobbies that produce wares, let them sell them and donate the money to a charity or use it for a class project.

3. Set up an International Club in your classroom.

4. Find out what collections children around the world value.

5. Have a T-shirt day where all students wear a shirt that they (or a family member or friend) has purchased from a place they've visited.

6. Let students earn points which they can use to buy attendance at a bonus afternoon event. During this event, students will be allowed to bring a game from home to share with two or three other students. Instead of letting them choose their playmates, have them draw names and change games periodically.

7. Have a music session where students who play instruments bring them in to demonstrate. Let the students explain the instruments, and if classmates are interested, they can divide into groups and try to learn the basics of each one.

8. Start a GOOD NEWS Club. Students can try to find good things that happen at school or in the neighborhood during the week. If you wish, you may even start a newsletter to spread the good news. *Use the reproducible worksheet on page 88 for this activity.*

9. Let your students bring in samples of their hobbies or materials from the clubs they're in to share with the class.

10. Lead a discussion on the important qualities it takes to be a good club member. Many of these stan-

dards are the same qualities it takes to be a good friend.

Suggested Children's Literature

The following list of children's books will enhance the focus of this lesson.

Grades K - 3

- *Two Good Friends* by Judy Dalton. Crown, 1974.

- *The Girl Who Loved the Wind* by Jane Yolen. Crowell, 1972.

- *Friend Is . . .* by Mark A. Taylor. Standard Pub., 1987.

- *Friend Comes to Play* by Nicoletta Costa. Putnam Pub. Group, 1984.

Grades 4 - 6

- *The Kid's Earth Handbook* by Sandra Markle. Atheneum, 1991.

- *Talking With Artists* by Pat Cummings. Bradbury, 1992.

- *On Their Toes: A Russian Ballet School* by Ann Morris. Atheneum, 1991.

- *Friend Indeed* by D. J. Arneson. Watts, 1981.

- *Friends* by Rosa Guy. H. Holt & Co., 1973.

Name ______________________________

GOOD NEWS CLUB

Think of something positive that happened at school or at home. Write an article for the GOOD NEWS club newsletter.

____

____

____

____

____

____

____

____

____

____

____

Hobbies My Partner Likes

Lesson 8 Interview

1. Do you have a hobby? What is it?

2. Do you belong to a club? What kind of club? Do you have meetings?

3. Do you take any special lessons outside of school?

   Music _______ Sports _______ Skating _______ Dance _______

   Art _______ Gymnastics _______ Other _______

4. Do you collect anything? Stamps _______ Coins _______ Dolls _______

   Stuffed Animals _______ Baseball Cards _______ Shells _______

   Rocks _______ Stickers _______ Posters _______ Other _______

5. Do you play a musical instrument? What is it?

6. What instrument would you like to play?

7. Do you like to make things? Knit _______ Crochet _______ Sew _______

   Woodwork _______ Models _______ Inventions _______ Other _______

8. What are your favorite games or toys? Who do you like to play them with?

Here are three hobbies (or games) we both like to do.

____

____

____

Hobbies My Partner Likes

Lesson 8
Art

Materials Needed: 2 pipe cleaners, glue, colored pens or pencils, scissors, construction paper scraps, pencil.

Directions:

1. Use the information from the interview to decide on four things that your partner likes best. Are any of these activities or hobbies that you like?

2. How can you show these hobbies in a drawing? Here are some ideas:

   a. If your partner likes to collect stamps, you might draw a postage stamp.

   b. If your partner likes to do needlepoint, maybe you could ask him or her to give you a small sample to put in the banner.

3. Do some thinking before you start. Make sure you have four ideas of interests or hobbies your partner likes before you start working.

4. Take two pipe cleaners, cross them and glue them down inside the banner on your artwork page.

5. In each of the four boxes show one activity that your partner likes to do. You can draw it with markers or colored pencils. You may also use colored paper to make your design. You may cut pictures out of magazines.

6. Each of the boxes should have a different picture.

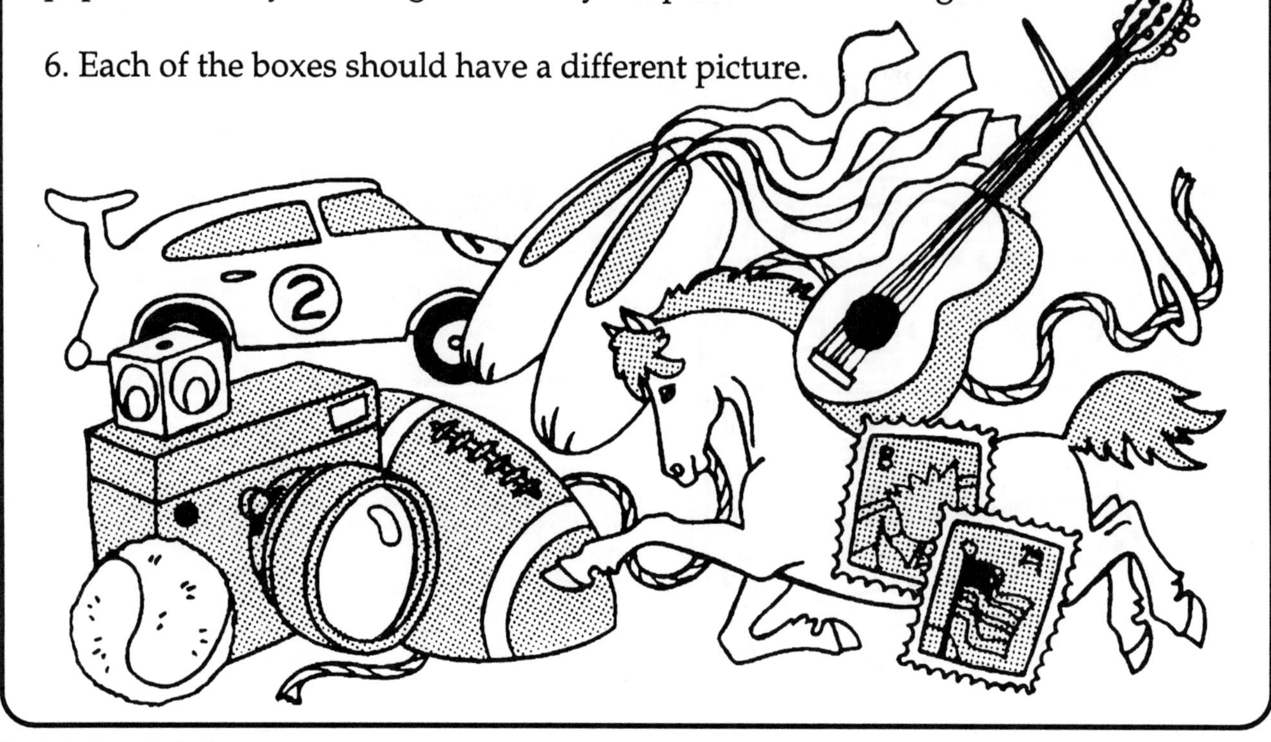

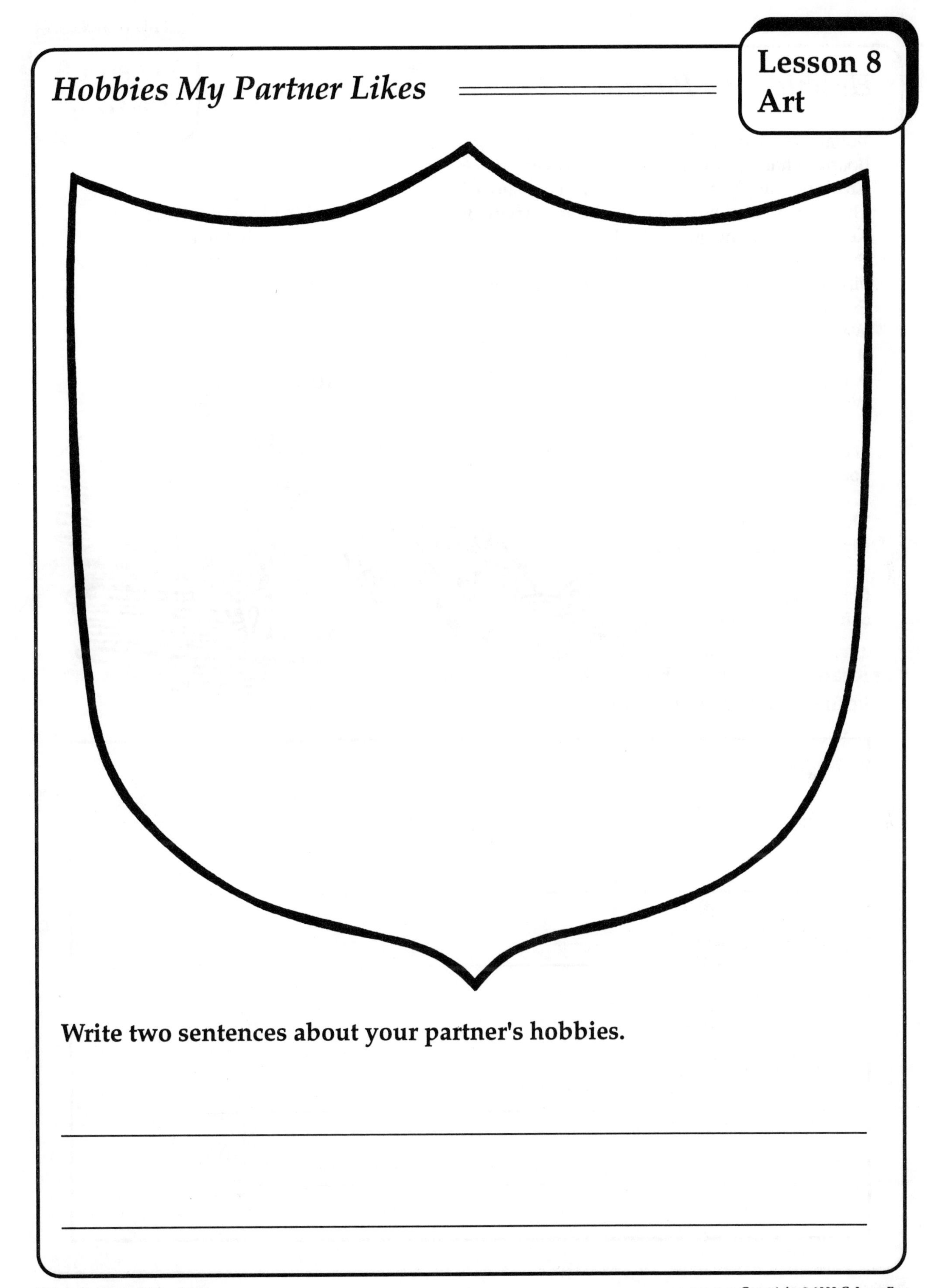

Hobbies My Partner Likes

Lesson 8
Art

Write two sentences about your partner's hobbies.

Hobbies My Partner Likes

Lesson 8
Writing

Boogie Boarding
Board in hand, I race down to the waves,
Crashing into the frigid water. The cold shock hits.
The ever-present breakers are blockers, trying to
Keep me from the quarterback,
But I charge through.
Finally I'm free, out where the waves start breaking.
Everyone is lined up, as if it were a giant race.
Waiting for the big one.
"It's coming," yells someone. I look back and see it.
A large wrinkle in the ocean.
We are paddling furiously.
It comes and I'm on top, higher than anybody.
I come slicing down the smooth green curl of water,
Soaring in toward the distant shore,
A cowboy on a wild bronco bucking and tossing.
The crowd scatters before me.
My flight ends on the foamy beach.

Chad Petty
San Diego, California

Hobbies
Save a coin
Collect a stamp
Travel to places on a map.
These are only three;
But there are hobbies from A to Z,
So I'm going to find one
Just right for me.

Gordon Settle
La Mesa, California

Read the poems. Then write a short story about your partner doing his or her favorite hobby.

____

____

____

____

____

____

Lesson 9: Halloween Fun

Overview and Objectives

Halloween is one of the most exciting days of the year for children. It is truly "their day." Lesson 9 takes advantage of the holiday setting and its strong appeal to students. In some ways, the day after Halloween is even better than the actual holiday. There is so much for children to share.

The students like talking about the innocent tricks they played as much as the treats they got. The excitement of the holiday becomes a good motivator for the students to discuss their mutual experiences. Not only does Halloween bring fun, it sometimes provokes fear. It is a holiday that encompasses a wide range of powerful thoughts and emotions for children. The children should discuss their feelings of this holiday as well as the goodies they received.

Although it is not necessary to do so, you may delete this lesson if you implement this program in the spring.

The feelings students have about Halloween or any other holiday do not come alive just on that one day, but can be expressed any time throughout the year.

Lesson Format

Discuss the interview questionnaire and the artwork directions with the students. Make sure all the materials are available. Each student will need a small lunch bag. Show a sample of the finished art project so the class will know what it should look like.

Remind the students to write two sentences at the bottom of the artwork page telling what their partners think about Halloween. Allow the glue on the artwork pages to dry overnight before placing them in the Partner Books.

The writing page includes poems written by other students. Ask the children to read the poems aloud to each other and then write a scary Halloween poem for their partners.

Enrichment and Multicultural Activities

The following activities are designed to promote multicultural awareness, encourage cooperative learning, and incorporate the friendship-building process into an integrated learning curriculum.

These ideas can be used to enhance the lesson for the partners as well as the whole class. All the activities relate to the topic of the lesson.

1. Have the children find out if other countries celebrate Halloween and if not, what major holidays they do consider important. Encourage the students to share what they know or have found out through their reading about celebrated days in other countries.

2. Some children do not celebrate certain holidays because of religious convictions. Discuss with the students the ways they might show respect for a classmate's beliefs by making this holiday more neutral and nonoffensive. For example a fall festival could be held instead of a Halloween Fair or costumes could be designed for a play rather than for the holiday.

3. Have students research the origins of Halloween. It was begun as All Hallow's Eve by Pope Gregory to honor the saints who had died and was often called "All Saints Day." Poor parishioners dressed up as saints and that's how costumes became a part of the celebration.

4. Have students dress up one day as a famous person from another culture or race (e.g. Mother Teresa, Martin Luther King, Gandhi).

5. In many places around the world, people collect money for UNICEF at Halloween time rather than asking for treats. The children could make this a class project. For more information contact: UNICEF, 331 E. 38th St., New York, N.Y. 10016.

6. Conduct a discussion about "tricks." Discuss what is appropriate and good clean fun as well as what is hurtful and destructive.

7. Brainstorm with the class what it would be like if there was no Halloween. What could happen to cause this?

8. Have the students make puppets showing what they will look like in their costumes. Students who are going to have similar costumes, such as a fairy princess or a scary monster, could work together in groups.

9. Provide the materials for a class mural on Halloween. The students can use pipe cleaners for stick bodies and torn tissue paper for costumes. Have each child put his or her partner in the mural and when it is com-

plete, have a contest to see which students remember what their classmates will be dressed as, on Halloween.

10. Play a guessing game. When each student comes in the door after lunch, tape or pin a picture of a Halloween character to his or her back. *Cut out the cards on reproducible page 96 and use them for this activity.*

Each student must guess what Halloween character is on his or her back by asking questions that can only be answered by a "yes" or a "no."

Suggested Children's Literature

The following list of children's books will enhance the focus of this lesson.

Grades K - 3

- *Halloween* by Joyce K. Kessel. Carolrhoda, 1980.
- *Witches, Pumpkins, and Grinning Ghosts* by Edna Barth. Clarion, 1972.
- *The Halloween Party* by Lomzo Auduron. Scribners, 1974.
- *The Witch Family* by Eleanor Estes. Harcourt, 1960.
- *Tell Me Mr. Owl* by Doris Van Liew Foster. Lothrop, 1957.

Grades 4 - 6

- *Meet the Witches* by Georgess McHargue. Lippencott, 1984.
- *All About Ghosts* by Christopher Maynard. Usborne, 1977.
- *The Hairy Horror Trick* by Scott Corbett. Little Brown, 1969.

mouse
ghost
robot
dragon
clown
astronaut
Dracula
witch
skeleton
jack-o'-lantern
black cat
Frankenstein

Halloween Fun

Lesson 9
Interview

1. How will you dress on Halloween?

2. Where do you go trick or treating?

3. What are some of your favorite candies or goodies to receive?

4. Do you have a jack-o-lantern for Halloween? Do you help make its face?

5. Which Halloween scary character do you like best? Witch _______

   Ghost _______ Spider _______ Goblin _______ Monster _______

   Black Cat _______ Dracula _______ Other _______

6. What should you do if you get an unwrapped piece of candy in your bag?

7. Have you ever played a trick on anyone while trick or treating? How did they feel?

8. What if you got a lot of candy and your little sister or brother didn't get very much? What would you do? Why?

9. How could you make your own costume so you wouldn't have to buy one?

10. If you could dress up as any character you wanted to be, what would you be? Why?

We both like these three things about Halloween.

____

____

____

Halloween Fun

Lesson 9
Art

Materials Needed: small paper bag, scissors, glue, tissue paper, colored paper scraps, yarn or string, old buttons and bows, pencil.

Directions:

1. What does your partner want to dress like on Halloween? You will be making a puppet like your partner's costume.

2. You will have to make the facial features somewhat flat. You could make a pointed nose that folds onto the puppet's face. However, the facial features you choose cannot stick out because you will not be able to close the book.

3. You will decorate the paper bag to look like your partner's costume. The head of the puppet will be made on the bottom of the bag. The bottom of the bag should be folded down over the front of the bag.

(bottom)

4. Cut a design such as points or scallops along the bag's open end. You might cut scallops if you are making a fairy princess. For a dragon you might choose pointed tips for a collar.

5. Using colored construction paper and/or tissue paper make eyes, a mouth, a nose, ears and hair for the puppet. Don't forget the whiskers on a cat!

6. After you have finished decorating the front of the bag, staple your puppet into your book. If the person you give the book to wants to remove the puppet to play with, this can be done easily.

Halloween Fun

Lesson 9
Art

Write two sentences telling what your partner thinks about Halloween.

Halloween Fun

Lesson 9
Writing

Read each poem. Then write a scary Halloween poem for your partner.

Halloween
It was a cold October night
If I remember right.
It was the 31st by date
The hour 12 midnight.
A lonely witch was traveling
On her journey to the moon,
When she crashed into the Satellite
And "busted" her poor broom.

Eric Beheim
San Diego, California

Trick or Treat
The winds sweep down
Through Grady house ruin;
Kicking shutters ajar
Catching cattails in bars
We shiver, we stalk
We cry out in fright
But trick or treat
Is only one night!

Kent Taylor
El Cajon, California

Halloween — Is It Real?
Pumpkins, witches, goblins
We imagine them so often,
But on Halloween
We see them as the real thing.

Margo Taylor
El Cajon, California

Lesson 10: Sports My Partner Likes

Overview and Objectives

Most children enjoy at least one sport either as a participant or as a spectator. Because sports are usually fast-paced, high-energy activities, the topic can generate interesting conversations between children. How can anyone talk about a homerun slide with two outs in the last inning without showing some excitement?

Many of the students will be knowledgeable about the same sports teams and what is happening to them at the school, community, college, city, or national levels. Team loyalty can be a good foundation for building new friendships.

Discussing sports is a good way for all of the students to get to know each other even better, but is particularly important for the student who performs poorly academically yet excels in sports. If a special education student does well in a popular sport, the class will probably be aware of this fact. However, if a student is an excellent gymnast, equestrian, or bowler, the class sometimes doesn't know this. If you discover that some of your students do have experience in less common sports, encourage them to explore these areas further with their partners. It is important to a child's self-esteem to be recognized for his or her talents, whatever they may be.

Even the students who do not actually play any sports will enjoy talking about the games they watch. Let the children know they don't have to play a sport to enjoy it.

Lesson 10 not only helps the youngsters discover information about their partners' sports interests, it also requires them to make some physical contact, which should take the embarrassment out of physical contact.

Lesson Format

Tell the class that they will be making six sports characters, using their partners thumbprints, on the artwork page. The students will show each character doing a sport their partner likes.

Go over the interview questionnaire and the artwork directions with the students. Elicit the names of some sports teams with which the students are familiar, and write the names on the board so the students will have a reference list for the interview page.

Show the students how to make a thumbprint and then turn it into a figure doing a sport. The examples on the direction page will be good idea starters, but the children should be encouraged to come up with their own ideas.

Have the students add the details to the thumbprints in pencil first and then carefully go over their pencil marks with marking pens.

Remind the students to write two sentences at the bottom of the artwork page telling about their partners' interest in sports.

The writing page includes poems written by other students. Ask the children to read the poems aloud to each other, find a sports picture in a magazine or newspaper that shows one of their partners' favorite sports, and write a description of what is happening in the picture.

Enrichment and Multicultural Activities

The following activities are designed to promote multicultural awareness, encourage cooperative learning, and incorporate the friendship-building process into an integrated learning curriculum.

These ideas can be used to enhance the lesson for the partners as well as the whole class. All the activities relate to the topic of the lesson.

1. Have students talk about the reason that the Olympic games are played. The discussion can lead to the importance of world peace.

2. Ask the students to draw the flags of each country that enters the Olympics. Encourage a wide variety of nations to be represented in this flag-making project.

3. Learn what sports are played in another country. Invite someone of that nationality to visit the class and demonstrate how the games are played.

4. Discuss famous athletes who have overcome barriers (e.g. women, people with disabilities, and those from a low socio-economic background).

5. Have students develop a bulletin board entitled "Children's Hall of

Fame." Let them bring in photos from books, magazines, and newspapers that portray children from around the world playing sports.

6. For an art lesson, divide the class into small groups and have each group make a different kind of oversized ball (e.g. soccer ball, basketball, tennis ball, handball, golfball, baseball, kick ball) out of butcher paper or large sheets of newsprint.

Cut out two circles for each ball and color or paint in all the appropriate details. Staple the edges of the two circles together except for a six-inch portion. Stuff the balls with crumpled newspaper or shredded material and then staple the six-inch area shut. Hang the completed balls from the ceiling as a mobile or display them in the corner of the room on the floor or on a table.

7. Play a game called Committee Ball. Divide the class into two teams. When the game is played, all the members of the kicking team run the bases together every time the ball is kicked. Don't keep score. Afterwards, discuss how it feels to play a game and not have any losers and how it feels to allow everyone to participate. This can be a lot of fun.

8. Have every child name their favorite sport, so the students can find out more about their commonalities. If some of the children like a sport that is not familar to the rest of the class, ask those students to tell about it.

9. Divide the class into small groups and assign a major sports team to each group. Have the members of each group keep the class posted as to what is going on with that team (e.g. their wins or losses, names of players added to the team, best team player, etc.). Use the team names in classroom activities.

10. During recess or PE, have the children play a sport where everyone has the same physical limitation. For example:

- Play wastebasket ball and require everyone to shoot while sitting down.

- Play baseball using the hand that is not normally used. Right-handed children would use their left hands and vice versa.

- Play a game where everyone is blindfolded so they can't see or where everyone wears earmuffs so they can't hear.

Later, talk about the difficulties encountered while playing these games.

Suggested Children's Literature

The following list of children's books will enhance the focus of this lesson and help students examine the feelings and challenges that other young people face.

Grades K - 3

- *Play Ball Zachary!* by Muriel Blaustein. Harper & Row, 1988.
- *Fox Under First Base* by Jim Lotimer. Scribners, 1991.
- *Sports Cars* by Sallie Stephenson. Capstone Print, 1989.
- *Sports Jokes* by Gary Chmielewski. Rourke Corp., 1986.
- *A Million Fish . . . More or Less* by Patricia C. McKissack. Knopf, 1992.

Grades 4 - 6

- *Thank You, Jackie Robinson* by Barbara Cohen. Lothrop, 1974.
- *Jim Thorpe* by Thomas Fall. Crowell, 1970.
- *Winners Never Quit* by Nathan Aaseng. Lerner, 1980.
- *Sluggers* by George Sullivan. Atheneum, 1991.
- *Sports Pages* by Arnold Adoff. Lippencott, 1990.
- *Superbowl Upset* by Maggie Twohill. Bradbury, 1991.
- *Brother of the Hero* by Lem Abramovich Kassil. Braziller, 1968.
- *Lucky Swim* by Matt Christopher. Little Brown, 1970.
- *Taking Sides* by Gary Soto. Harcourt, 1992.
- *Yang the Youngest and His Terrible Ear* by Lensey Namioka. Little Brown, 1992.

Lesson 10
Interview

Sports My Partner Likes

1. What sports do you like? Baseball _______ Skating_______

   Swimming _______ Gymnastics _______ Basketball _______

   Tennis _______ Bowling _______ Soccer _______ Other _______

2. Do you go bike riding? How many speeds does your bike have?

3. Do you or does someone in your family have a skateboard?

4. Do you like to exercise?

5. What sports equipment do you have at home?

6. What do you like to do during P.E. or recess?

7. Have you gone to any sports events? Yes _______ No _______

8. Do you watch sports on TV? Yes _______ No _______

9. Which team is your favorite? _______________

10. Are you on any team at school or in your neighborhood? What position do you play?

11. Do you have a favorite sports star? Who is he or she?

12. Does anyone else in your family play a sport? Who? Which sport?

Here are three sports activities we could do together.

____

____

____

Sports My Partner Likes

Lesson 10
Art

Materials Needed: inkpads, thin-line markers, paper towels, colored pencils, pencil.

Directions:

1. Think of all the sports that your partner likes to play or to watch.

2. Put your partner's thumb on the ink pad. Now press your partner's inked thumb *very gently* on the artwork page. Put one thumbprint in each of the boxes.

3. Have your partner clean his or her thumb well with a damp paper towel. Be careful not to get ink on your clothes or papers.

4. Using your pencil, make little characters out of the prints. See the examples below for ideas. Each of your characters should be doing a sport that your partner likes.

5. Write over the pencil marks with a thin-line marker. You can also use colored pencils.

6. Color in the background or draw in the equipment needed to play the sport. For example, you could draw a swimming pool or a tennis court.

Sports My Partner Likes
Lesson 10
Art
2
5
Write two sentences about your partner and sports.

Sports My Partner Likes

Lesson 10
Writing

Read each poem. Then find a picture in a magazine or newspaper which shows one of your partner's favorite sports. Write about what is happening in the picture.

____

____

____

____

____

____

Swimming
Diving, diving to and fro.
Don't stop now, there's not far to go!

Somersault here, somersault there,
Somersault everywhere.

Handstands up, handstands down,
Handstands all around!

But when you think you're having fun,
You may be getting too much sun!

So put on lotion quick, quick, quick,
Before the sunburn makes you sick!

Swimming is a pastime, swimming is neat,
But after you get out you'll have cold feet!

Tamara Falicov
San Diego, California

Surfing
Riding on waves with the greatest of ease,
First on your stomach, then to your knees,
Under a curve and over a swell,
Then you are down, and they hear you yell.
Then you come in to take in the sun.
A day at the beach can really be fun.

Laura Baz
San Diego, California

Lesson 11: Liking Ourselves

Overview and Objectives

The next five lessons are designed to encourage the partners to discuss their feelings. Lesson 11 focuses on feelings that students have about themselves.

It's always hard to talk about ourselves without sounding very conceited or overly humble. The questions and activities in this lesson will help students identify their positive qualities and share them with their partners. Lesson 11 gives students an opportunity to talk about what makes them special without the risk of sounding like they are bragging. More importantly, it encourages the children to discuss their feelings about their own self-image.

Everyone has trouble opening up to others. Children become embarrassed or uncomfortable because they are afraid that sharing feelings makes them vulnerable. However, they will need to get by this barrier if they are to develop a meaningful friendship. Positive things usually occur in a relationship where people are open, but there is always a risk that one person will use the other's feelings and secrets to hurt him or her. Because of this risk, it is important for you to spend a little extra class time setting the stage for this lesson.

Getting Started

Before the interview, art, and writing sessions begin, allow your students to discuss their fears about sharing feelings. You can use the enrichment and multicultural activities listed in this lesson or refer to one of the many books on the market which include ideas for discussions about emotions.

Tell the students they are going to make silhouettes of their partners' heads and then create a list of words which say nice things about them.

Have your students make their silhouettes before they begin the lesson. See the first four artwork directions for specific steps to follow. You will need to set up two or three places in the room where your students can work on the silhouettes, and you will need to schedule the use of the lamps or overhead projector.

Lesson Format

Read the interview questions aloud to your students. Take some extra time to discuss what it was like to tell their partners about themselves.

The class will need more time than usual for the interviews. Encourage extra discussion beyond just answering the assigned questions. Expressing personal feelings is an important landmark in a friendship and shouldn't be hurried.

Review the remaining artwork directions with the students. Since the children have already made their silhouettes, they only have to glue them onto the artwork page. Then they can concentrate on filling in the words about their partners.

The words should be complimentary and written on the outside border of the artwork page. It would be helpful to write a class-generated list of complimentary words on the board. Encourage older children to use a dictionary or thesaurus for this activity. Remind the students to write two complimentary sentences at the bottom of the artwork page about their partners. Put some sentences on the chalkboard as idea starters.

1. _______ likes to be _______.
(hugged, told stories, smiled at, etc.)

2. _______ feels happy when someone tells him or her _______ .

3. _______ sees himself or herself as _______, _______, _______ .
(use positive adjectives)

4. _______ feels good when he or she does a good job such as _______ .

The writing page includes poems written by other students. Ask the children to read the poems aloud to each other and then write a poem about feelings they have in common.

Enrichment and Multicultural Activities

The following activities are designed to promote multicultural awareness, encourage cooperative learning, and incorporate the friendship-building process into an integrated learning curriculum.

These ideas can be used to enhance the lesson for the partners as well as the whole class. All the activities relate to the topic of the lesson.

1. Brainstorm with the class how people express feelings of sadness,

(crying, acting gloomy or moody, getting sympathy from adults or friends, needing hugs, isolating themselves, acting grumpy or angry), and how people express happiness (laughing, smiling, hugging, sharing, complimenting, giving love or affection).

2. Discuss how different cultures express their feelings of sadness and happiness.

3. Have students write a story, poem, or essay on how they feel about world peace. Encourage them to tell what people could do to contribute to harmony among all humankind.

4. Ask students to discuss what it would feel like to be in a country where they could not speak the language. Discuss how they could communicate in other ways.

5. Make class mobiles with the word "LOVE" written in different languages.

6. Make a bulletin board where students are asked to post good things about the "featured student of the week."

7. Pin a piece of paper on the back of each class member. Have the students go around the room and write one thing they like about each person on the papers. Since the children can't see what anyone is writing on their own backs, they should be more open about expressing their positive feelings. Variations of this idea include:

- Have the students write down one physical feature they like about that person, or one word that describes a time when they think that person is happiest (e.g. recess, music time, weekend, etc.).

- Have the children write one nice thing that person has done for them during the year.

- Draw names to decide who will write on whose back — this will cut down on time needed for this activity.

8. Start a new way of communicating in the class. Ask the student to send Feeling-Grams to each other. They can make mailboxes especially designed for the Feeling-Grams.

9. Begin each day with an open-ended sentence for your class to discuss. Some examples are:

- I feel loved when ____________.

- I feel happy when ____________.

- I feel lonely when ____________.

- I like to daydream about ________.

10. Play some of the games sold by

the Ungame Company: Ungame, Social Security, or Roll-a-Role.

Suggested Children's Literature

The following list of children's books will enhance the focus of this lesson and help students examine the feelings and challenges that other young people face.

Grades K - 3

- *Don't Look At Me: A Child's Book About Feelings* by Doris Sanford. Mautnomah Press, 1986.
- *Duck Takes Off* by Susanna Gretz. Macmillan, 1991.
- *Brice's Mice* by Syd Hoff. Harper & Row, 1988.
- *Roommates and Rachel* by Kathryn O. Galbraith. Collier, 1991.
- *Willie's Not the Hugging Kind* by Joyce Durham Barrett. Harper-Collins, 1989.

Grades 4 - 6

- *Seeing in Special Ways: Children Living with Blindness* by Thomas Bergman. Gareth Stevens, 1989.
- *On Our Own Terms: Children with Physical Disabilities* by Thomas Bergman. Gareth Stevens, 1989.
- *Anna, the One and Only* by Barbara Joosse. Lippincott, 1988.
- *Children of the Fire* by Harrietta Robinet. Atheneum, 1991.
- *Fair Maiden* by Lynn Hall. MacMillan, 1990.

Liking Ourselves

Lesson 11
Interview

1. What is one thing you like about yourself? Why?

2. What is one thing you like about me? Why?

3. Describe yourself to me. Use both physical and feeling words.
   Examples: tall, fun, happy.

4. Tell one thing someone has done to help make you happy.

5. Tell one thing someone has done to make you unhappy or upset.

6. How do you feel when someone gives you a compliment?

7. How do you like others to show you that they like you?

   Tell you ______ Listen to you ______ Smile at you ______

   Hug you ______ Give you a pat on the back ______ Other ______

8. What are you feeling right now?

9. Tell one nice thing that happened to you today or yesterday at school.

10. Think of three nouns that tell about you.
    Example: a girl, a friend, a writer.

Here are three things we both like about ourselves.

____

____

____

Liking Ourselves

Lesson 11 Art

Materials Needed: lamp or overhead projector, 8-1/2 X 11 piece of black construction paper, scissors, glue, pencil, and markers.

Directions:

1. Ask your partner to sit in a chair with the side of his or her face toward the wall.

2. Tape the black paper to the wall or chalkboard behind your partner's head. Shine a lamp at his or her head, so that you can see a silhouette on the paper. Make sure your partner's silhouette fits on the paper. You can move the paper or lamp around to make it fit.

3. Trace around the silhouette on the paper with a pencil. Take your time and go very slowly. You want to make a profile outline of your partner's face. Include your partner's neck and a bit of collar if there is room on the paper.

4. Cut out the outline with scissors.

5. Glue the silhouette on your artwork page.

6. Think about your interview. What does your partner like about himself or herself? What do you like about your partner? Write five or more nice words about your partner around the outside of the silhouette that you have glued on the artwork page for today's lesson.

7. Make sure your spelling is correct before writing the words. Use a dictionary if you need to.

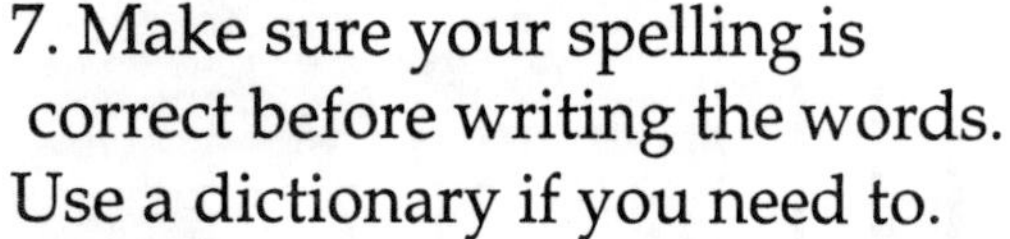

Liking Ourselves

Lesson 11
Art

Write two sentences that compliment your partner.

Liking Ourselves

Liking Yourself
Life is like a player piano,
Where each key, black or white,
Plays its own special, unique note.

Jane Brucker
La Mesa, California

Read each poem. Then write a poem about some feelings both you and your partner have in common.

____

____

____

____

____

____

A Feeling
When I am happy, I like to talk
To whomever I pass when I go for a walk.
I like to dance
Or read of romance,
Or ride around
And paint the town.
I like to sing a beautiful song
That I would not sing when things go wrong.
I like to party all week through,
When the nights turn black and the days turn new.
But the thing I do most, and it's really snappy,
Is admire myself when I am happy.

Levan Cruz
San Diego, California

When you look at me,
I am black,
as a race is.
When you see me,
I am me,
as only I am.

Donna Bryson
San Diego, California

Lesson 12: Thanksgiving

Overview and Objectives

Thanksgiving Day is the beginning of a special holiday season. People's thoughts turn to home and family, near or faraway. There is a festive atmosphere everywhere. Family get togethers, music, good food, and thankfulness are all part of the traditions at this time of the year.

Unfortunately, the holidays are not happy times for everyone. The festive celebrations can make children who have difficult or chaotic home lives feel that they are the only ones who are uncomfortable about their family gatherings.

Lesson 12 deals with both the good and bad feelings that come with the holidays. This lesson stresses similar experiences, while also allowing the expression of varying emotions. Having the partners share their feelings should help the students who are depressed, and may enable them to find some things, people, or experiences which really are worth being grateful for. As a teacher, you can help students understand both their joy and their sadness. It is an important lesson for all.

Getting Started

Before the interview, art, and writing sessions begin, discuss what Thanksgiving means to people. Talk about the good and bad points. Discuss why people might become depressed around the holiday time and how they could deal with their feelings in a constructive manner.

Emphasize that it is not bad to be unhappy during a holiday. Encourage your students to begin thinking about how people who are happy can share their joy and good fortune with others.

Lesson Format

Review the interview questions and the art directions with the class. Tell the children they will be making a "friendly" turkey, with their partners' help. The students will use their partners' left hand to draw a pattern for the turkey. Be sure they understand how this is done.

On the chalkboard, illustrate how to trace another person's hand, reminding the children that they must let the thumb point toward the right side of their Partner Books.

Elicit from the class a list of things that people could be grateful for, and write them on the board. Instead of writing two sentences at the bottom of the artwork page as they usually do, the students will write words that tell what their partner is grateful for.

The words will be placed inside each of the four tail feathers of the handprint turkey. Remind the students to have their partners sign their first name at the bottom of the artwork page.

The writing page includes poems written by other students. Ask the children to read the poems aloud to each other and then write a Thanksgiving poem with their partners (e. g. one poem per set of partners).

Enrichment and Multicultural Activities

The following activities are designed to promote multicultural awareness, encourage cooperative learning, and incorporate the friendship-building process into an integrated learning curriculum. These ideas can be used to enhance the lesson for the partners as well as the whole class. All the activities relate to the topic of the lesson.

1. Thanksgiving means "being thankful" and "giving to self and others." Discuss how other cultures demonstrate gratitude and generosity.

2. Ask students to brainstorm all the useful things that other cultures have given to the United States (e.g. spaghetti from the Italians, clocks from the Swiss, sausage from Germany).

3. Dramatize ways people can show generosity without sharing money or things. Ask the children how they can give of themselves (e.g. from smiles and handshakes to time and service).

4. Invite the students to bring in different spices from around the world. Have everyone smell or taste the spices and discuss how they are used and where they originated.

5. Have students share an unusual dish their family has for Thanksgiving Day dinner or a special tradition their family follows on this holiday.

6. Put on a puppet show about the Pilgrims and Indians. Have the children show puppets that are both happy and sad at the first Thanks-

giving. Let the class think about ways for those puppets that are happy to help the unhappy ones.

7. Help the students develop a bulletin board which illustrates why they are thankful for each classmate. This is a good opportunity to acknowledge the personal achievements and improvements the children have made since the beginning of the year.

8. Thanksgiving is a family-oriented holiday. The traditional feast symbolizes unity. Ask the students to prepare a turkey dinner in the classroom with the help of their parents and then share it together. This may be the only opportunity the children have to enjoy a traditional Thanksgiving meal.

Because this activity involves menu planning, it can be part of the health lesson. The cooking portion will reinforce math skills through measuring ingredients, estimating portions, and enlarging recipes.

9. Brainstorm with the class to think of some inexpensive menus that could be used as alternatives for the Thanksgiving Day meal.

It is a good opportunity to dispel the myth that everyone eats a feast on Thanksgiving. Economically underprivileged children need to know that there is nothing wrong with the foods they use to celebrate. It's the meaning that really counts.

10. Show a film, video, or filmstrip about Thanksgiving. Two filmstrips that are good are entitled: *Thanksgiving for a King* and *The First Thanksgiving*.

Suggested Children's Literature

The following list of children's books will enhance the focus of this lesson.

Grades K - 3

- *The Bears Find Thanksgiving* by John Barrett. La Fave Co., 1986

- *Pilgrims & Thanksgiving* by Rae Bains. Troll Assoc., 1985.

- *Bear's Thanksgiving* by Bobby Marilue. Oddo Publishing, 1978.

- *The Thanksgiving Mystery* by Joan Lowery Nixon. Simon & Schuster, 1979.

- *A Charlie Brown Thanksgiving* by Charles Schulz. Random House, 1974.

Grades 4 - 6

- *Refugees* by Derek Heater. Rourke Enterprises, 1989.

- *Cranberry Thanksgiving* by Maude Devlin. Parents Magazine Press, 1977.

- *The Plymouth Thanksgiving* by Leonard Weisgard. Doubleday, 1967.
- *No Company Was Coming to Samuel's House* by Dorothy Corey. Ethridge Books, 1976.
- *Jimmy & Joe Have a Real Thanksgiving* by Sally Glendinning. Garrard, 1974.

Thanksgiving

Lesson 12 Interview

1. What are your favorite foods to have for Thanksgiving Dinner?

2. Do you have dinner at home or go to someone else's home on Thanksgiving Day?

3. Do you help cook anything for the Thanksgiving dinner? What is it?

4. What do you do after you eat dinner?

5. What is your favorite thing about Thanksgiving?

6. Name four things that you are thankful for.

7. If you could change one thing about this holiday, what would it be and why?

8. What do you think it would be like to be alone for Thanksgiving?

9. How can you help someone who isn't happy or has no one with whom to share Thanksgiving Day?

10. Finish the following sentences:

    I feel good when . . .
    I feel lonely when . . .
    I feel needed when . . .
    Thanksgiving Day makes me feel . . . because . . .

Feelings we share about Thanksgiving.

____

____

____

Thanksgiving

Lesson 12
Art

Materials Needed: your partner's left hand, colored pencils or crayons, toothpicks or pipe cleaners, glue sticks, pencil, pen, and markers.

Directions:

1. Place your partner's left hand on the artwork page.

2. Make sure his or her thumb is closest to the right side of the page.

3. Trace around his or her fingers very carefully. After your partner picks up his or her hand, finish the palm so that it is rounded.

4. Draw an eye, a beak and two small sacs hanging from the turkey's throat. The thumb should look like the turkey's head.

5. The four fingers will be the turkey's tail feathers.

6. Think about the things your partner said he or she was thankful for. Write one on each of the finger-feathers.

7. Lightly color each feather a different color. Make sure you can still see the words you wrote earlier. You may wish to use a pen or marker.

8. Color the body of the turkey brown. You can draw in the design of the feathers on the body if you like.

9. Now make the turkey's legs and feet. You can draw them or glue on toothpicks to make them look three-dimensional.

10. Have your partner sign his or her name to the Happy Thanksgiving Greeting at the bottom of the artwork page.

I'M THANKFUL WE HAVE FOOD TO EAT BUT MOSTLY I'M THANKFUL FOR:

Happy Thanksgiving from ______________________________

Thanksgiving

Lesson 12
Writing

Read each poem. Then write a Thanksgiving Day poem for your partner.

Thanksgiving
Butterball turkey, all basted and brown,
All of your aunts and uncles in town,
Football, parades and maybe fresh snow;
All these are part of the Thanksgiving I know.

Potatoes, squash, and pumpkin pie,
Grandpa telling stories with
A twinkle in his eye,
Holiday faces all aglow;
All this is part of the Thanksgiving I know.

Like Pilgrims and Indians
Together we eat,
Everyone in their own special seat,
Too soon it's over,
And we're all sad to go;
All this is part of the Thanksgiving I know.

Jane Brucker
La Mesa, California

Let us be thankful that there still is sunshine,
That we still can glimpse the blue of the sky
and in our onward way,
continue to look up.
Let us be thankful for friends with
kindly smile and cheerful words.
This is a time for grateful Thanksgiving!

Unknown

Lesson 13: Wishes, Dreams, and Changes

Overview and Objectives

Nothing shows quite as much of our inner selves as our wishes and dreams. Sharing them is a courageous act of friendship. Lesson 13 gives the partners a chance to not only talk about their wishes and dreams, but also to discuss the things they are not pleased with and would like to change.

The interview questions are designed to allow the students to reveal only as much about themselves as they choose. Some children will be insightful and find it easy to be open, while others will have a difficult time sharing their faults or misgivings.

Observe this activity very carefully. It will reveal how the students view themselves in relation to the world around them. More specifically, the responses will let you know which students believe they are in charge of their actions, and which students rely on others to make decisions and changes for them. You can follow up with individual support and/or counseling, as needed.

Getting Started

Before you begin the interview, art, and writing sessions, introduce the concept of wishing wells and what they symbolize. Discuss the following topics:

- other good luck symbols.
- the difference between luck and hard work.
- what a person can do to control situations which need to be changed (e.g. share and discuss the problem, remain calm, think, do not take failure as a direct reflection of personal worth, etc.).

To get the students thinking about making wishes, ask them what they would wish for the entire class if they were granted three wishes from a fairy godmother or a genie. Write the wishes on the chalkboard.

Lesson Format

Explain to the students that they are going to make coins to put in the wishing well illustrated on the artwork page. If possible show a sample of a completed page. Review the interview questions and art directions with the class.

> **Note:**
> If magazines and newspapers are available, have the children cut out small pictures or words that show what their partners would like to have, be, or change. Let the children know that they can glue these pictures or words on the coins instead of writing words.

Remind the students to write two sentences about their partners' wishes and dreams at the bottom of the artwork page. Allow the glue on the artwork pages to dry overnight before placing them in the Partner Books.

The writing page includes poems written by other students. Ask the children to read the poems aloud to each other and then think of three wishes they would like to grant to their partners.

Enrichment and Multicultural Activities

The following activities are designed to promote multicultural awareness, encourage cooperative learning, and incorporate the friendship-building process into an integrated learning curriculum.

These ideas can be used to enhance the lesson for the partners as well as the whole class. All the activities relate to the topic of the lesson.

1. Do a journal-writing activity where students enter their wishes and dreams for making a better world for ALL people.

2. Ask students to research good luck symbols from various cultures. Ask those children who have good luck pieces or charms (e.g. rabbit's foot, four-leaf clover, articles of clothing, lucky pennies) to bring them to the classroom for sharing.

3. Have each student cut out shamrocks from green paper. The children could write about a wish for making the world a more loving place to be. Younger students could illustrate their ideas and paste them on the shamrocks. Make a bulletin board that has a rainbow on it. The youngsters staple their shamrocks at the bottom of the rainbow to symbolize the treasures one can find at the end of a rainbow.

4. Have the students look in the newspaper and find one or two people who have made important

changes in the world. Ask the class to identify the changes these people have made and tell whether they think their accomplishments were good or bad. Encourage the children to give reasons for their opinions.

5. Discuss with the children how they could make life better for another person or for their partners.

6. Make a Feelings Circle out of poster board. When students come into the classroom in the morning, they can identify their moods by placing a clothespin with their name on it by the word on the Feelings Circle that expresses how they feel.

The Feelings Circle should have the phrase "I am feeling . . . " in the middle of it and emotion words such as: angry, silly, stubborn, excited, happy, sad, disappointed, tired, and grouchy around the outside border.

During the morning warmup time, let the children who share the same feelings get together and talk a few minutes.

This activity can be good for the students who are already having a bad time, because it will help them get their feelings out in the open instead of carrying them around all day. It also alerts you to those children who may need extra encouragement or attention during the day.

7. For creative writing exercises have the students complete the following sentences:

- If I were a color, I'd be ________.
- If I were the principal for a day, I'd ________.
- If I am good, my parents will ________.
- If I were Superman or Superwoman, I would ________.
- If I started a new planet, the people would ________.
- I would do this to make a better world: ______. This is why______.

8. Make collages from magazine pictures of both good and bad things in the world. Afterwards, discuss the pictures in the collage and talk about how the children can change or improve the problem areas.

9. Have the children show anger, love, sadness, and other feelings during art time using clay and fingerpaints to make abstract forms or shapes.

10. Start a self-improvement unit in the class. Have each student choose something about himself or herself that needs improving and then outline the steps needed to change.

Suggested Children's Literature

The following list of children's books will enhance the focus of this lesson and help students examine the feelings and challenges that other young people face.

Grades K - 3

- *The Dream* by Dr. Stephen Timm. Touchstone, 1982.
- *Rainbow Rider* by Jane Yolen. Thomas Y. Crowell, 1974.
- *Dreamcatcher* by Audrey Osofaky. Orchard Books, 1992.
- *I Need a Lunch Box* by Jeannette Caines. Harper & Row, 1988.
- *The Auction* by Jan Andrews. MacMillan, 1991.

Grades 4 - 6

- *Refugees: Search for a Haven* by Judith Bentley. Messner, 1986.
- *Human Rights* by John Bradley. Gloucester Press, 1987.
- *Sadako and the Thousand Paper Cranes* by Eleanor Coerr. Putnam, 1977.
- *The Big Book for Peace* by Ann Durell and Marilyn Sachs (eds). Dutton Children's Books, 1990.
- *Windcatcher* by Avi. Bradbury, 1991.
- *Savina, The Gypsy Dancer* by Ann Tompert. Macmillan, 1991.

Wishes, Dreams, and Changes

Lesson 13
Interview

1. If you had three wishes what would they be and why?

2. Who do you look up to in school?
   Who do you respect in your neighborhood?

3. If you could change how you look, what would you change and why?

4. The best thing that could happen to you is . . .

5. What do you daydream about?

6. If you could be older or younger, which would you be and why?

7. If you were a color of the rainbow, which one would you be and why?

8. If you could change how others treat you, what would you change?

9. Finish these phrases:

   I can't . . .   I can . . .
   I won't . . .   I will . . .
   I don't . . .   I do . . .

10. What would you like to be when you grow up?

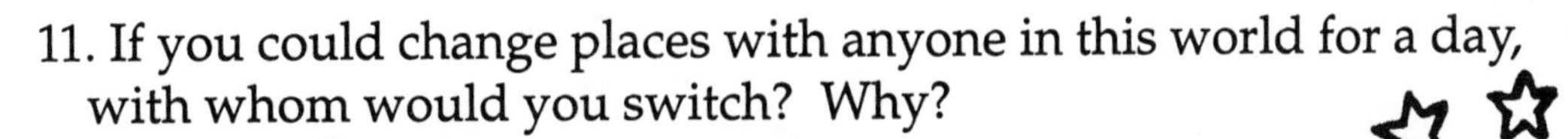

11. If you could change places with anyone in this world for a day, with whom would you switch? Why?

Here are three wishes and dreams we both have.

____

____

____

Wishes, Dreams, and Changes

Lesson 13
Art

Materials Needed: scissors, crayons and colored pencils, glue sticks, pencil.

Directions:

1. Think about the things your partner would like to change. Think about three wishes he or she would like to come true. Check with your partner to see if he or she agrees.

2. Write your partner's three wishes on the coins below.

3. Color the coins lightly so that you can still see the writing.

4. Cut out the three coins.

5. Color the wishing well and the background of the picture on the artwork page.

6. Glue the three coins on the wishing well.

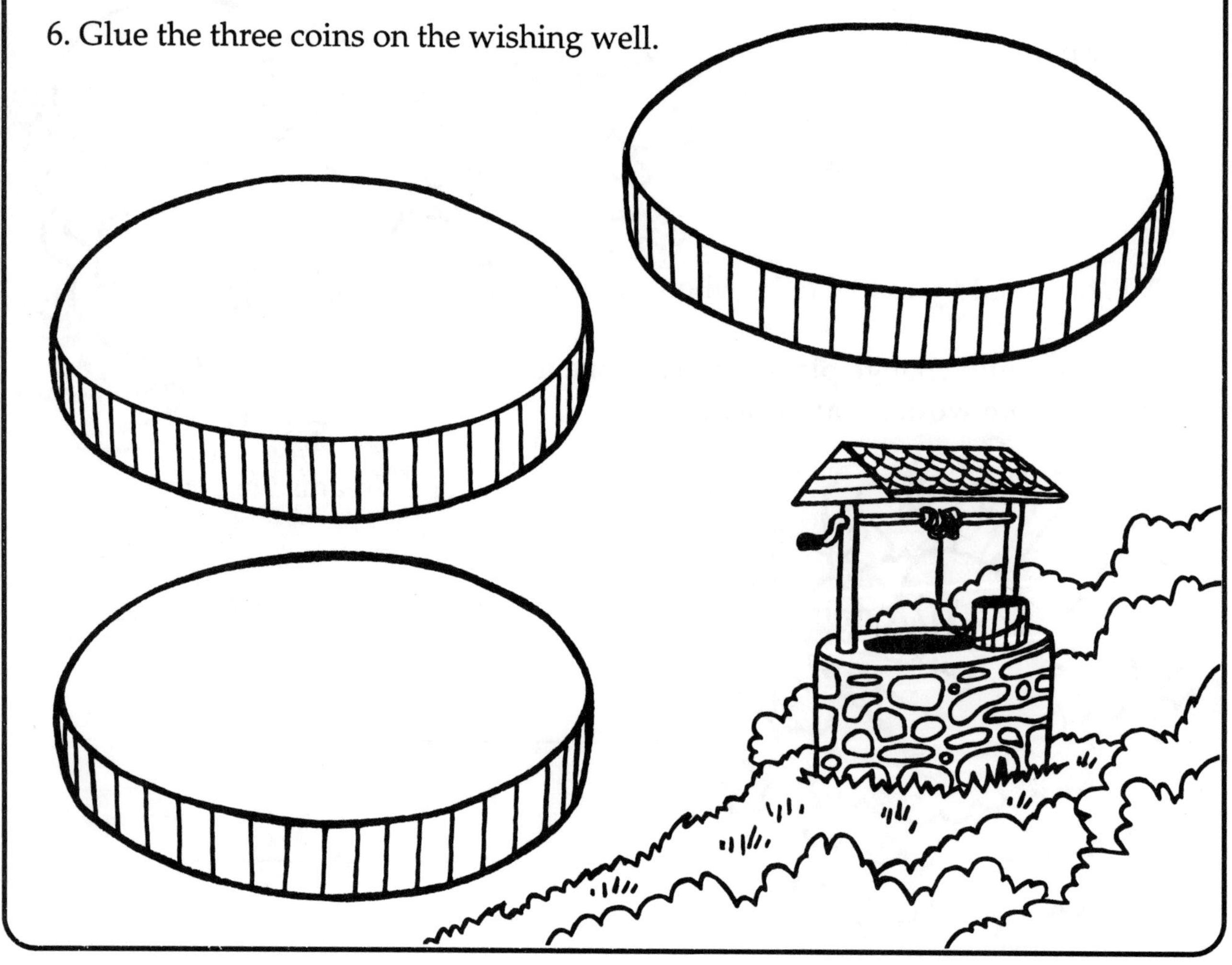

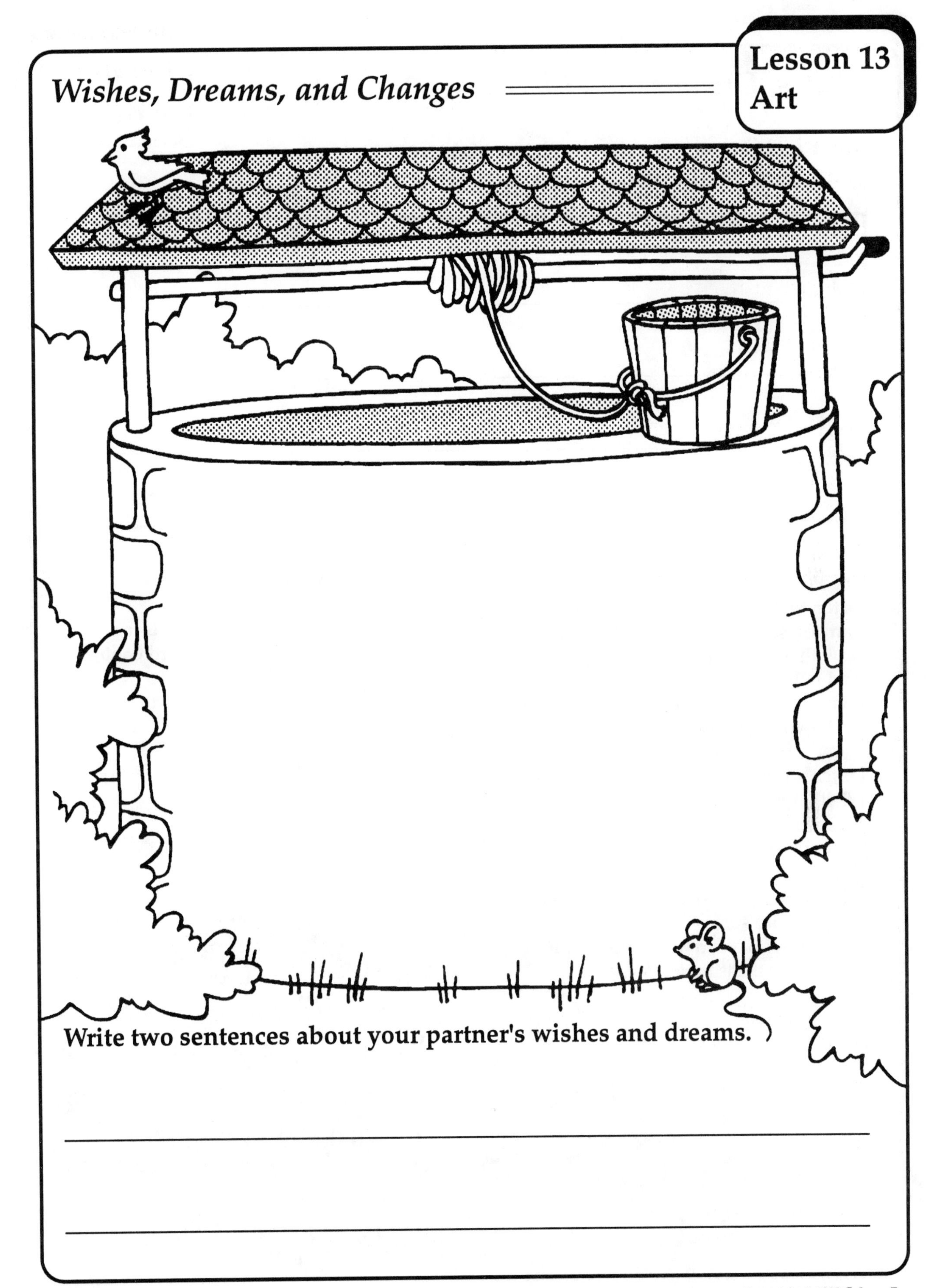
Wishes, Dreams, and Changes
Lesson 13
Art
Write two sentences about your partner's wishes and dreams.

Wishes, Dreams, and Changes

Lesson 13 Writing

Read each poem. Then write three wishes you would grant to your partner.

1. ______________________________

2. ______________________________

3. ______________________________

The Future
Listen to the rustling of the leaves,
Can you see
How they are swaying, silently
And falling with ease?
I wish our world could do things like that
And if you don't agree with me,
I'll eat my hat!!
I often wonder how the future will be,
Whether we will be riding rockets,
spaceships,
Or tiny little peas!
When we grow up we shall surely see!
But you know we shouldn't be weeping
with sorrow,
We will just have to wait until the future
awakens tomorrow.

Tamara Falicov
San Diego, California

Wishes
Anyone can wish,
But only few come true,
But if you wish hard enough,
Someday, sometime
It might . . . come true.

Jeff Martin
La Mesa, California

Lesson 14: Friendships

Overview and Objectives

Just imagine what life would be like without friends — pretty lonely and dull. Unfortunately, many children have few, if any, friends. Beyond being shy, some children may not understand what is expected in a friendship, how friends act, what they do or don't do.

Trustworthiness, honesty, concern, and sharing are just a few of the qualities a person needs in order to develop and maintain a friendship. Lesson 14 deals with the friendships the partners already have, while revealing what characteristics both partners value in a new or old relationship. Hopefully, this lesson will encourage students to think about what it really means to be a friend and help them learn to better meet each other's needs.

After working together for the past thirteen weeks, many of the partners, but not all, will have become friends. The circle of friends on the artwork page is a good visual aid to prompt students to think about friendship as a continuous process between many different kinds of people.

Lesson Format

Let the students know that in this lesson they will complete a picture of children, from around the world, who are joining their hands in friendship. Discuss the interview questionnaire and the artwork directions with the children.

Discuss the significance of people from many different racial and cultural backgrounds being friends. If there is time, have the class name different nationalities they know about and locate the country or continent of origin on a world map or globe.

Ask all of the children to write their first names on the chalkboard. Tell your students to use these names to label the children in the circle of friends. If a classmate looks like or reminds them of one of the children in the circle, they can use that student's name.

Remind the students to write two sentences at the bottom of the artwork page telling about what their partners think is important in keeping good friendships.

The writing page includes poems written by other students. Ask the children to read the poems aloud to each other and then write a poem about friendship.

Enrichment and Multicultural Activities

The following activities are designed to promote multicultural awareness, encourage cooperative learning, and incorporate the friendship-building process into an integrated learning curriculum.

These ideas can be used to enhance the lesson for the partners as well as the whole class. All the activities relate to the topic of the lesson.

1. Ask the children to write to a pen pal who lives in another country. For names and addresses contact: World Pen Pals, 1690 Como Ave., St. Paul MN 55108.

2. Many cities have a "sister" city in another part of the world. Contact the local Chamber of Commerce and ask for a speaker to visit the class. The guest can let the class know more about this sister city program.

3. Let several students present a conversation without using words. Tell them that only facial and body movements can be used to convey what they want to say to each other.

4. Teach your class the sign language for the deaf, showing them the words for certain feelings such as: love, friendship, anger, sadness, etc.

5. One part of friendship is to accept people for who they are. Let the class know there are many things that make up who a person is. Racial or ethnic identity, gender identity, abilities or limitations are but a few. Ask each student to share what is special about his or her own identity.

6. Show films, filmstrips, or videos that deal with friendships and human values.

7. Have your students talk about why they should feel safe with certain people and not with others. Ask the children to define trust and discuss why it is important in any friendship.

8. Create a new holiday. Have a FRIENDS DAY. Let each of your students invite a schoolmate who is also a friend to class. They can introduce the student to the whole class and tell about their friend's favorite interests or hobbies.

9. Have the whole class draw names for secret pals. Each student must do one nice thing a day for his or her secret pal. Everyone must work hard to keep the person from finding out who is doing the nice things.
The children can use the reproducible sheet on page 136 for sending a special note to their secret pals.

At the end of the week, have a discussion about what it was like to be on both sides of the experience — both from the giver and receiver's viewpoint.

10. Make posters for a FRIENDSHIP WEEK. Each poster should illustrate one or more of the important aspects of friendship.

Suggested Children's Literature

The following list of children's books will enhance the focus of this lesson and help students examine the feelings and challenges that other young people face.

Grades K - 3

- *We Are Best Friends* by Aliki. Greenwillow Books, 1982.
- *Earl's Too Cool For Me* by Lia Komaiko. Harper & Row, 1980.
- *Let's Be Enemies* by Janice May Udry. Harper and Row, 1961.
- *Periwinkle* by Rober Duvoisin. Knopf, 1976.
- *Peter's Long Walk* by Lee Kingman. Doubleday, 1953.

Grades 4 - 6

- *The Secret Grove* by Barbara Cohen. Union of American Hebrew Congregations, 1985.
- *The Hundred Dresses* by Eleanor Estes. Harcourt, 1944/1974.
- *Feelings About Friends* by Linda Schwartz. Learning Works, 1988.
- *Feelings: Everybody Has Them* by Stephanie Neuman. SNB Pub., 1984.

Cut out the Secret Pal card. Fold it in half. Write a note to your secret pal on the inside of the card. Give it to your secret pal when he or she is not looking.

Friendships

Lesson 14 Interview

1. Who is your best friend in school?
   Why do you like this person?

2. Name three other people you like. Why do you like them?

3. Who is your best friend in your neighborhood?
   Why do you like this person?
   Do you think this person likes you as a best friend?

4. What three things make you like someone?

5. When do you like to be with your friends?
   When do you like to be alone?

6. How do you show your friends that you like them?

7. How do you feel when a friend wants to play
   with someone else and not you?

8. Do you ever get mad at your friends? Why?

9. Do your friends ever get upset with you? Why?

10. When do you feel shy around other people?

11. If you could be anyone's friend in class,
    who would it be and why?

Here are three things my partner and I feel are important to make a friend.

____

____

____

Friendships

Lesson 14
Art

Materials Needed: crayons or colored pencils, pencil.

Directions:

1. Look at the artwork page. You will see a picture of a circle of friendship. The children in this picture are from countries around the world. Look at each person's face.

2. There are two children that are not finished. Use your crayons or colored pencils to make them look like you and your partner. This will complete the circle of friendship.

3. Write your first names above your pictures. Keep the writing neat and small.

4. Color in all the characters. Think about the things that would make each of these children a good person to know as a friend. Discuss your ideas with your partner.

Friendships

Lesson 14
Art

Write two sentences about what your partner thinks is important for keeping a good friendship.

____

____

Friendships

Lesson 14
Writing

A Friend is . . .
A friend is someone that you like
Someone you can do things with
Like walk, run, or ride a bike.

A friend is someone who talks
And listens to you,
Who makes you laugh
When you are blue.

A friend is someone who's always there,
Someone to share with
And someone to care.

A friend is a neighbor, mother, cousin,
Schoolmate, teacher, or brother.
And a friend could be a newcomer, too
If you'd just smile and say
"How do you do?"

Jane Brucker
LaMesa, California

FRIENDS

Friendship
Friendship
lovely
delicate
fragile
Like a crystal glass
it holds so much
but is easily broken.

Freda Statom
San Diego, California

Read each poem. Then write a poem about friendship for your partner.

Lesson 15: Christmas and Hanukkah

Overview and Objectives

The Christmas spirit is infectious. Green and red begin to show up in decorations and displays everywhere, and smiling Santas appear in both malls and classrooms. Around the same time of the year, the blue and white colors of Hanukkah are seen, along with the six-pointed star and eight-candled menorah.

The holiday celebrations are supposed to be filled with "love and cheer," but for many children this is not the case. Hanukkah and Christmas can bring both good and bad feelings. Parents who are having trouble making ends meet may become overly sensitive or even hostile during the holidays because they feel uncomfortable not being able to give their children what they need or want.

In addition, many families have problems at this time of the year because their traditional gatherings result in arguments. Parents' frustrations are often transferred to their children who have trouble understanding these feelings. Children can feel the tension, but may not yet have learned how to cope with it in a constructive way.

It is important for students to be able to discuss both the good and bad sides of the holidays. They will watch television shows which show family stories ending in bliss, while their own lives do not. Students need to realize that everyone experiences both disappointment and joy, even during the holidays. Lesson 15 will show students how to explore both the bright and sad moments of Christmas and Hanukkah.

This lesson is also designed to show that children around the world celebrate an assortment of holidays which center around exchanging gifts and having family gatherings. In many cases, the holidays are tied to a religious belief, as Christmas and Hanukkah are. If you wish, you may include other celebrations by adding questions to the interview page.

Getting Started

Discuss the meaning of Christmas and Hanukkah with the children. Jewish students in the classroom will appreciate the opportunity to share their holiday with others who may not be familiar with Hanukkah. If there are youngsters in the classroom from other cultures, help them share their traditions too.

Lesson Format

Explain to the class that they will be using the outlines of their partners' hands to make a holiday greeting that symbolizes the joining of hands of children all over the world. Discuss the interview questionnaire and the artwork directions with the students.

The artwork concept is simple. It requires that the students draw four overlapping hands. However, some students may have a figure-ground perception problem and find this task challenging. Let them draw two overlapping hands and use a different skin color for each hand.

Under the hands, the students should write the holiday greeting their partners select. Put these sample greetings on the chalkboard:

- **Peace and Love to All**
- **Happy Holidays to You**
- **May Your Holiday Be Bright**

Add your own greeting idea or let the children make suggestions. Remind the students to write two sentences at the bottom of the artwork page telling what their partner wants to give and receive for the holidays.

The writing page includes poems written by other students. Ask the children to read the poems aloud to each other and then describe a wonderful gift they think their partner would like to receive. Remind them that gifts are not always "things." For example, love and peace top the list of the best gifts.

Enrichment and Multicultural Activities

The following activities are designed to promote multicultural awareness, encourage cooperative learning, and incorporate the friendship-building process into an integrated learning curriculum.

These ideas can be used to enhance the lesson for the partners as well as the whole class. All the activities relate to the topic of the lesson.

1. Get some pictures from the library which show children celebrating holidays all over the world. Discuss the similarities and differences in these holidays. Talk about the feelings children have when celebrating holidays.

2. Learn holiday songs from around the world. Compare the lyrics and discuss the meanings.

3. Have students discuss ways they can give to other peoples and countries. Make a universal holiday card on which children can share their ideas.

4. This time of the year is a good opportunity for the class to give something back to the community. As a class, decide on a project that would benefit the neighborhood (e.g. donating to a food bank, planting flowers, cleaning up a street or park).

5. Plan a field trip to visit a home for the elderly or the children's ward of a hospital.

6. Have your students bring in old Christmas or Hanukkah cards. Talk about the pictures and symbols on the front of the cards. Discuss the meanings of the different greetings and verses. Have your students cut off the fronts of the cards and make a collage that represents the feelings of each child. Let the children sign their names and display the finished project in the hall to share with the rest of the school.

7. Explain that compliments are gifts. Many students may not know what to do or say when they receive a compliment. Experiment with different role-playing situations where children can practice accepting compliments, gifts, and thank you's.

8. For a creative writing exercise, have the students answer this question: If you could give your family members anything in the whole world, what would you give and why?

9. Have a gift-giving project where all the classmates bring in toys for needy children who may not receive anything for the holidays. The toys can be used, but should be clean and in good condition. Have students wrap the toys in class during an art project.

10. Have each student make a gift for one of their classmates. Let the children draw names. Explain that the gift must be something creative, made from recycled or inexpensive materials. Gifts can be a card, poem, drawing, or homemade item.

Suggested Children's Literature

The following list of children's books will enhance the focus of this lesson and help students examine the feelings and challenges that other young people face.

Grades K - 3

- *A Picture Book of Hanukkah* by David A. Adler. Holiday House, 1982.

- *Holiday Treats* by Esther Hautzig. Macmillan, 1983.
- *The First Christmas* by Robbie Trent. Harper & Row, 1990.

Grades 4 - 6

- *Christmas Time* by Gail Gibbons. Holiday House, 1982.
- *The Hanukkah Book* by Marilyn Burns. Four Winds, 1981.
- *The All-Around Christmas Book* by Margery Cuyler. Holt, 1982.
- *Around the Table: Family Stories of Sholom Aleikem* edited by Shevrin Aliza. Scribners, 1991.
- *The Truth About Santa Claus* by James Giblin. Crowell, 1985.
- *A Child's Christmas in Wales* by Dylan Thomas. Holiday House, 1954.

Christmas and Hanukkah

Lesson 15
Interview

1. What do you want for Christmas or Hanukkah? Name three things.

2. What would you feel like if you didn't receive the gift you wanted?

3. How would you feel if you got what you wanted, but your brother or sister did not?

4. Do you put up a Christmas tree? Yes ______ No ______

5. Do you help decorate the tree? Yes ______ No ______

6. If you celebrate Hanukkah, what kinds of decorations do you use?

7. How would you feel if you couldn't help decorate the tree or the house for the holidays?

8. Does your family get together to celebrate the holidays?

   Yes ______ No ______

9. When you go to bed at the end of this celebration day, how do you feel? What do you think about?

10. What gifts do you enjoy giving? What gifts do you enjoy receiving?

Here are three things we both like about the holidays.

____

____

____

Christmas and Hanukkah

Lesson 15
Art

Materials Needed: colored marking pens; crayons; thin-line red, green, and blue markers; pencil.

Directions:
1. Have your partner place one of his or her hands on the artwork page so you can trace around it. (Each partner must use a different hand. Decide which partner will use the left hand and which will use the right.)

2. Ask your partner to trace around one of your hands so that the two hands look like they are joined together. Look at the example below. If you have the room and time, trace two more hands so you have four overlapping hands.

3. Go over the hand patterns with marking pens or crayons. Use different colors to symbolize different colors of people's skins.

4. Ask your partner which greeting below he or she would like to use, or write your own. Copy the greeting onto the artwork page in pencil. Make sure it is neat. Now go over the pencil marks with red, green, or blue markers.

Christmas and Hanukkah

Lesson 15
Art

Write one sentence about what your partner wants for the holidays.
Write one sentence about what your partner wants to give to someone.

____

____

Christmas and Hanukkah

Lesson 15 Writing

Read the poems. Write down the steps you would follow to wrap a gift for your partner.

At Christmastime

At Christmas, these are
the things I know:
Fragrance of pine; air frosted
keen with snow;
Laughter of children, raised in
glad surprise;
Breathless expectancy; the smiling eyes
Of friends with gifts white-clad and
ribbon-tied;
Odor of good things cooking.
There abide.
The dearest things I know in all the earth;
Home, and the loved ones, friendship,
song, and mirth.

Unknown

Hanukkah

Hanukkah, Hanukkah
festival of lights
Hanukkah, Hanukkah
eight bright nights
Hanukkah, Hanukkah
when our rights were turned,
For our people who so yearned,
to worship God in their own way.
Hanukkah, Hanukkah
for peace we pray.

Jane Brucker
La Mesa, California

Lesson 16: Valentine's Day

Overview and Objectives

The Valentine is a classic symbol of love. For children, it is a less personal gesture of friendship and recognition. They like Valentine's Day for the pretty colors, the heart-shaped candy and cookies, and the fun cards they exchange. Lesson 16 builds on the feelings associated with Valentine's Day.

Lesson Format

Tell the children that the objective of this lesson is to make a valentine for their partners. Discuss the interview questions and the art directions with the children. Make sure all the materials for the art session are available. If possible, show the class a sample of a finished artwork project.

Let the students know that instead of writing two sentences at the bottom of their artwork pages, they will write a Valentine's verse to their partners. Remember to allow the glue to dry on the artwork pages before placing them in their Partner Books.

The writing page includes poems written by other students. Ask the children to read the poems aloud to each other and then write a short description for their partners about what Valentine's Day means to them.

Enrichment and Multicultural Activities

The following activities are designed to promote multicultural awareness, encourage cooperative learning, and incorporate the friendship-building process into an integrated learning curriculum.

These ideas can be used to enhance the lesson for the partners as well as the whole class. All the activities relate to the topic of the lesson.

1. Have a discussion about the saying: "Love Makes the World Go 'Round."

2. Ask students to make a list about how certain people in their community have shown them kindness and support. Encourage the children to

share their lists.

3. As a class, design a valentine for everyone in the world. The children can illustrate ways to solve many world problems (e.g. create peace, make a clean environment, provide plenty of food for all, etc.)

4. Valentine's Day is a good time to talk about gender equity and identity. Students might make a list of female and male role models who live in their community and then send each of these people a valentine card with a message of thanks.

5. Have students learn to say "I love you" in other languages. Don't forget sign language.

6. Divide the class into groups of four. Have the students work as a team to make small mailboxes for their desks to use on Valentine's Day. Let the teams compete for the most original, the most colorful, and the best team effort.

7. Conduct a cooking lesson. Arrange with the cafeteria staff to use an oven or bring an electric toaster oven with the capacity to bake a cake to the class. Divide the class into groups. Each group will be responsible for contributing to the making of a heart-shaped cake as part of the Valentine's Day refreshments. Partners can be assigned to work on each different step of the preparation (e.g. measuring the ingredients, mixing the ingredients, baking the cake, decorating the cake, writing a Valentine's greeting on the cake, preparing the punch, serving the cake, etc.). Don't forget to assign a clean-up crew.

Valentine Cake Directions:
Grease and flour an 8 x 8 square pan and an 8 inch round pan. Prepare cake batter from a package of white or chocolate cake mix. Divide the batter equally between the two prepared pans. Bake the square pan for 25-35 minutes, and the round pan for 30-35 minutes.

Place square cake on a large tray with one point towards you. Cut the round cake in half. Place the cut edge of each half against the top sides of the square to form a heart. Decorate the cake with a can of fluffy white frosting.

8. Provide the materials for each class member to make a valentine person to represent themselves. Prepare a bulletin board in the hallway, office, or cafeteria which sends a valentine message from the class to the other students in school.

9. Discuss how it feels to be "left out." Hold the discussion a few days before Valentine's Day. Talk about why people are left out and what the

students can do to cope with these feelings, as well as how to avoid making anyone in the class feel excluded. This may help prevent the students from playing favorites during their card exchange.

10. Ask the students to think of the special people who help them during the school day (e.g. custodial staff, secretary, nurse, librarian, principal, office worker, PTA president, bus driver, cafeteria worker, playground supervisor, crossing guard, teacher aide).

Write the names of these people on slips of paper and ask students to draw a name from a bag. Cards can be made for these workers and given to them on Valentine's Day. *The children can use the reproducible sheet on page 152 for sending a special note to one of these helpers.*

Suggested Children's Literature

The following list of children's books will enhance the focus of this lesson.

Grades K - 3

- *Love Is A Special Way of Giving* by Joan Walsh Anglund. Harcourt, 1960.
- *Hug Me* by Patti Stren. Harper & Row, 1977.
- *Arthur's Great Big Valentine* by Lillian Hoban. Harper Trophy, 1989.
- *Valentine Day: Things to Make and Do* by Rolyn Supraner. Troll, 1981.
- *Little Love Story* by Fernando Krahn. Lippincott, 1976.
- *Don't Be My Valentine* by Joan M. Lexau. Harper & Row, 1985.

Grades 4 - 6

- *Arthur's Valentine* by Marc Brown. Avon, 1980.
- *The Valentine Box* by Marjorie Thayer. Children's Press, 1977.

Color and cut the Valentine's Day card. Write a note on the inside to one of the special people who work at school and give it to him or her.

Valentine's Day

Lesson 16
Interview

1. What does Valentine's Day mean to you?

2. Has your class exchanged Valentines before?

3. Do you know a Valentine's verse or rhyme?

4. How would you feel if you didn't get a Valentine from a friend and you sent one to him or her?

5. Have you ever given a Valentine to a teacher? Who and why?

6. Do you make or buy your Valentines?

7. Why do you think someone might like a homemade Valentine better than one bought at a store?

8. Have you ever sent a Valentine card without signing your name? Were you embarrassed to do this?

9. Do you ever get candy for Valentine's Day?

10. Have you ever gotten anything besides cards and candy for Valentine's Day?

Here are three things we both like about Valentine's Day.

____

____

____

Valentine's Day

Lesson 16
Art

Materials Needed: crayons, markers, glue, red and pink construction paper, red and pink tissue paper, paper lace doilies, scissors, black thin-line marker, pencil.

Directions:

1. Cut out a big red or pink heart. Here's how to do it:

   a. Fold a piece of construction paper in half.

   b. Draw a half of a heart with your pencil, using the folded side as the center of the heart.

   c. Cut out the heart. Do *not* cut along the fold.

   d. Open the paper. It will be a complete heart.

2. Glue the heart on the artwork page. Around the edges do one of the following:

   a. Cut out the lacy part of a doily and decorate the edges of the Valentine with it.

   b. Use your pencil to make small flowers out of the red or pink tissue paper. Glue these small flowers around the heart to decorate it.

   c. Think of your own decoration. Be creative.

3. In the center of the Valentine, write a verse to your partner. Write in pencil first, check your spelling, and then trace over the verse with a black thin-line marker.

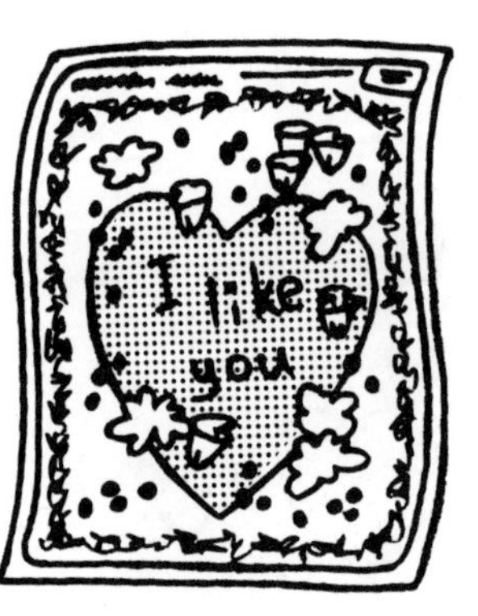

Valentine's Day

Valentine's Day

Lesson 16
Writing

Who Do I Love?
Who do I love
Now let me see . . .
Scott or Michael or Ronny?
Oh but no, there's not just three.

There's Kent and Corey,
And Mark and Bryan,
Bobbie and Donald
And Joel and Ryan.

Well that's not all
There's a whole lot more . . .
And that's what Valentine's
Day is for.

Jane Brucker
La Mesa, California

Somebody
Someone loves you deep and true
If I weren't so bashful
I'd tell you who.

Unknown

Read the poems. Write a short description for your partner about what Valentine's Day means to you.

Lesson 17: Birthday Celebrations

Overview and Objectives

Celebrating a birthday means having a cake with candles, listening to friends sing *Happy Birthday,* making wishes, and opening presents. Lesson 17 introduces a different way of celebrating birthdays. This lesson gives the students an opportunity to celebrate all of their birthdays at once. It's a special time they can all share and also feel good about themselves.

This will probably be the first time that students whose birthdays come during the summer or holiday vacations can celebrate with their classmates. The activities are designed to honor the individual child by giving recognition to the day he or she was born, and then turning the event into a special time that everyone can share by celebrating together.

Lesson Format

Explain to the students that they are going to celebrate their partners' birthdays by decorating the birthday cake that is illustrated on the artwork page. The material used for the decorations will depend on what is available in the classroom.

Read the interview questions and art directions aloud with the class. Remind the children to write a birthday greeting that includes their partners' name and date of birth. This information will go on top of the cake.

The students will write two sentences about what their partners have told them during the interview about their birthday. The sentences are written at the bottom of the artwork page. Allow the glue to dry on the artwork pages before they are placed in the Partner Books.

The writing page includes poems written by other students. Ask the children to read the poems aloud to each other and then compose a birthday party invitation for their partners.

Enrichment and Multicultural Activities

The following activities are designed to promote multicultural awareness, encourage cooperative learning, and incorporate the friendship-building process into an integrated learning curriculum.

These ideas can be used to enhance the lesson for the partners as well as the whole class. All the activities relate to the topic of the lesson.

1. Children all over the world celebrate their birthdays. Have students research what children from other countries like to do on their birthdays. Are there any special customs or celebrations they do that are not practiced in the United States?

2. Invite guest speakers from other countries to share what holidays they celebrate in their homelands.

3. During classroom or outside activities, have students line up by birthdate (e.g. June 22). Start with the beginning of the year and end with December. You may find some students who were born on the same day. It will be fun for children to discover this commonality. *For math practice, have the students use the reproducible worksheet on page 160 to make* a *birthday graph.*

4. Bring in calendars from around the world (e.g. Chinese calendar, Mayan calendar, Jewish calendar). Discuss the origin of the calendars and the meanings of the symbols on them.

5. Let the children find their birthday symbol and the symbol for each of their family members on a Chinese calendar and do research to find out about its significance.

6. At the beginning of the year, make a list of all of the students' names and birthdays. Have each student draw a name and be responsible for making the birthday student feel "special for that day."

If a student's birthday occurs on a weekend, it can be celebrated on the closest Friday or Monday. Children who have birthdays during the summer or holiday vacations can choose another day during the school year that will represent their birthday.

Put the birthdays on a calendar as a reminder and make a separate list for yourself showing which child is responsible for each birthday, in case the students need reminding later in the year.

7. Have the class make a giant birthday card every time a student has a birthday. All the students sign their names and write one thing they really like about the birthday child.

8. For an art lesson, have all the students who are born in the same

month make a mural that shows the things that happened during that month.

9. One day a month, for a one hour period, allow all of the birthday students to put on a party for the class. Let the students organize it by deciding what games will be played and what refreshments are needed. The other children should be responsible for cleaning up.

10. Have the students play games where they are teamed by their common birthday month. This will reinforce the idea of commonality to the children.

Suggested Children's Literature

The following list of children's books will enhance the focus of this lesson and help students examine the feelings and challenges that other young people face.

Grades K - 3

- *A Letter to Amy* by Jack Ezra Keats. Harper and Row, 1968.
- *Birthday Party (and Other Tales)* by Annie Ching. Asian American Bilingual Center (Berkeley), 1979.
- *Special Korean Birthday* by Jae Hyun Hahn and Hon Hahn. The Institute for Intercultural Studies (Los Angeles), 1980.
- *The Birthday Tree* by Paul Fleishchman. Harper Collins, 1979.
- *Dandelion* by Leo Leoni. Delacorte, 1974.
- *Oliver's Birthday* by Marilee Robin Burton. Harper & Row, 1986.

Grades 4 - 6

- *Let's Celebrate* by Caroline Parry. Kids Can, 1987.
- *Amazing Days* by Randy Harelson. Workman, 1979.
- *The Birthday Present* by Bruno Munari. World, 1959.
- *Don't You Remember?* by Lucille Clifton. Dutton, 1973.

Name ______________________________

BIRTHDAY GRAPH

Ask 10 people in class to tell you their birthday month. Fill in the graph below.

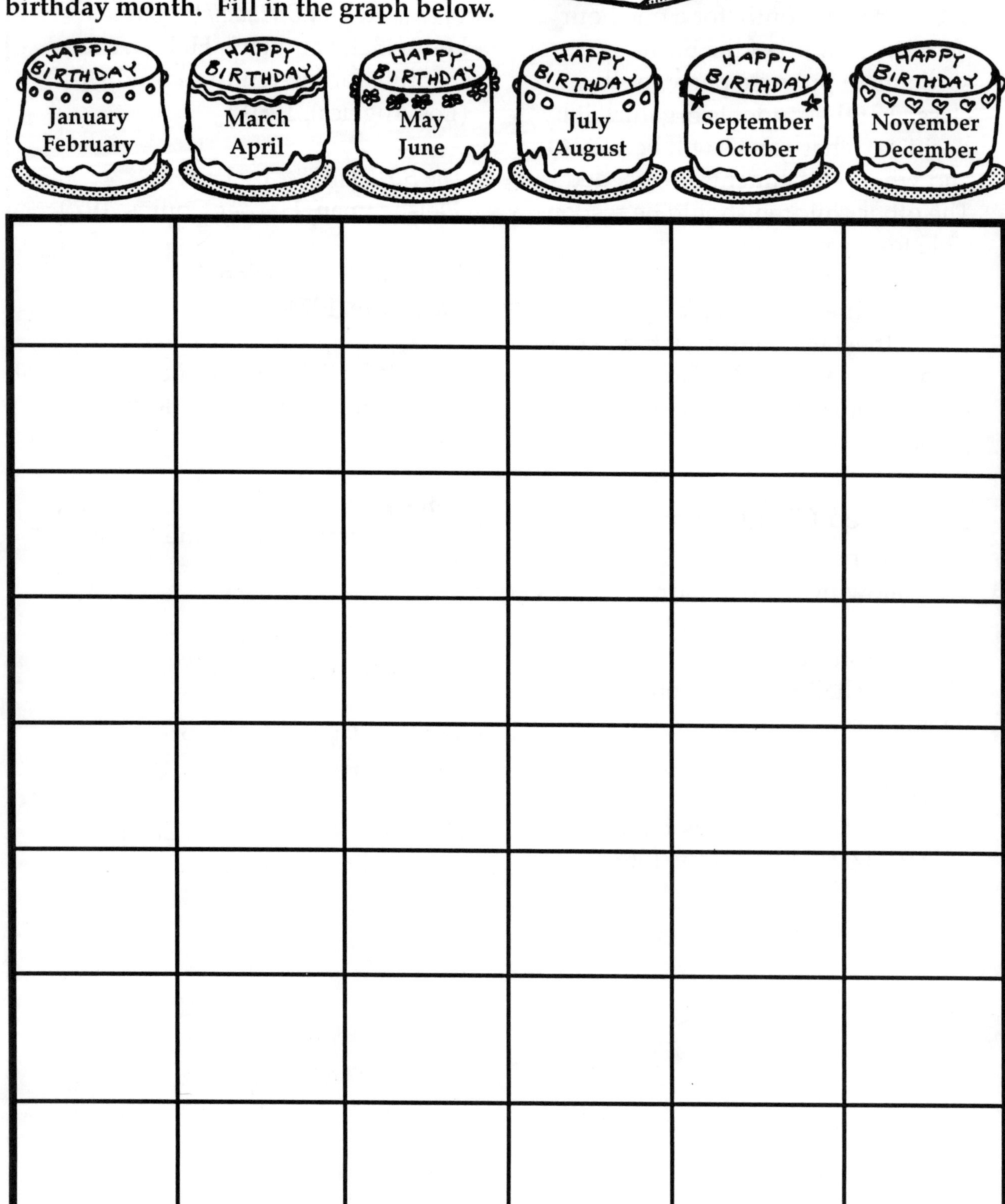

Birthday Celebration

Lesson 17
Interview

1. When were you born?

2. Where were you born?

3. How old are you now?

4. If you could have anything you want for your birthday, what would it be?

5. Is there anyone in your family who has a birthday during the same month as you?

6. Do you know if any of your classmates have a birthday in the same month as you do?

7. Tell about one of your best birthdays. Why was it good?

8. Can you think of anything bad about one of your birthdays?

9. What age would you like to be now and why?

10. What kind of birthday cake do you like best?

Here are three things we have in common about our birthdays.

____

____

____

Birthday Celebration

Lesson 17
Art

Materials Needed: glue, crayons, colored paper, tissue paper, pencil.

Directions:

1. Look at the cake on the artwork page. Think about the things that your partner likes and does for fun. Pick out one that would make a good decorating theme to use on the cake. Example: a cowboy theme, a hockey field, a doll house, a castle.

2. Use colored paper, tissue paper and/or crayons to decorate the cake. If you are using colored paper or tissue paper, cut all the pieces out first and lay them on the cake to make sure they fit. Then glue them down. If you are going to draw the decorations, draw them in pencil first so if you make a mistake, you can erase it.

3. Be sure you know how old your partner is. You will write this information in one of your sentences at the bottom of the page.

4. On the top of the cake write a Birthday Greeting including your partner's name and date of birth.

Birthday Celebration

Lesson 17
Art

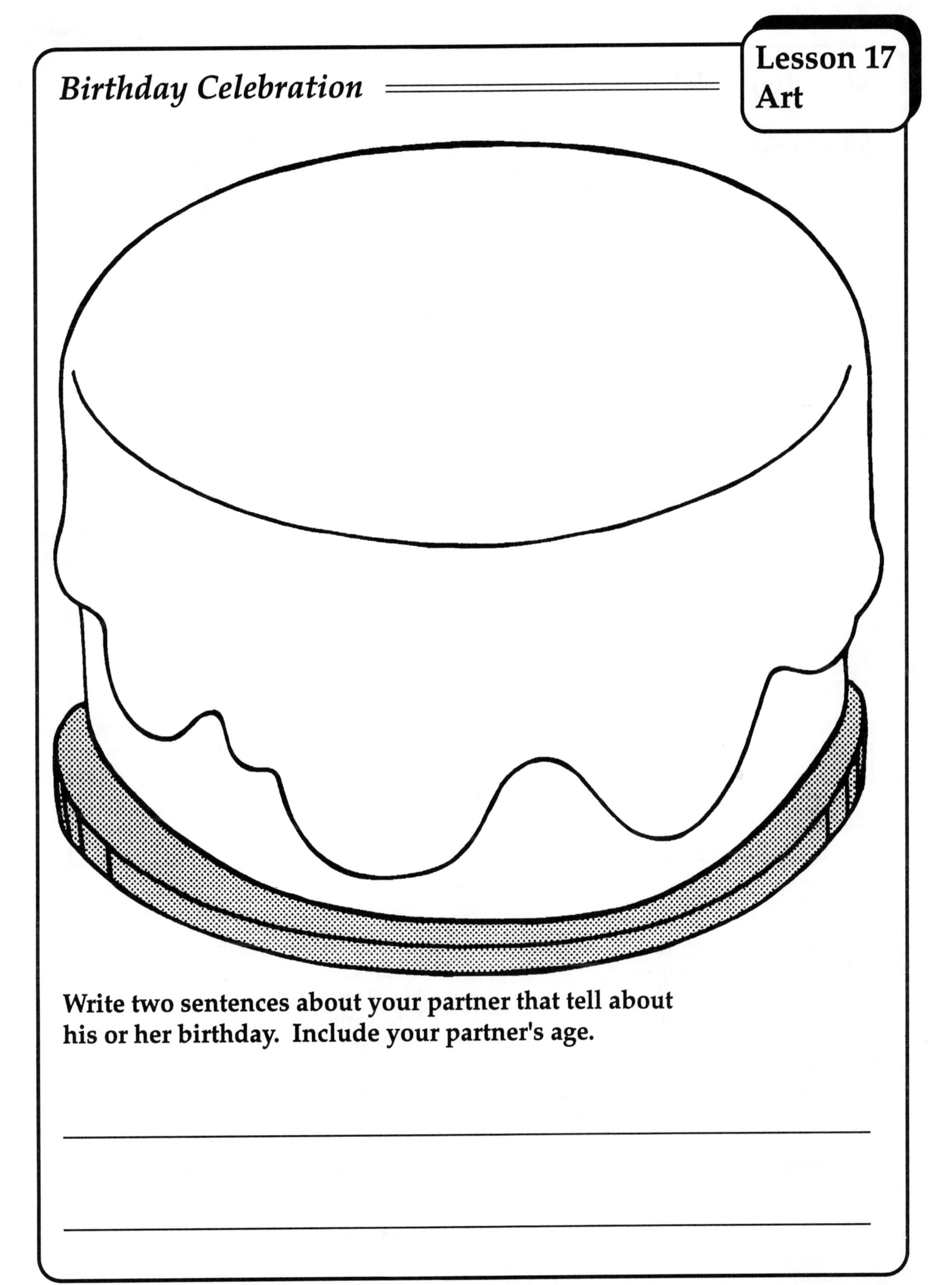

Write two sentences about your partner that tell about his or her birthday. Include your partner's age.

Birthday Celebration

Lesson 17
Writing

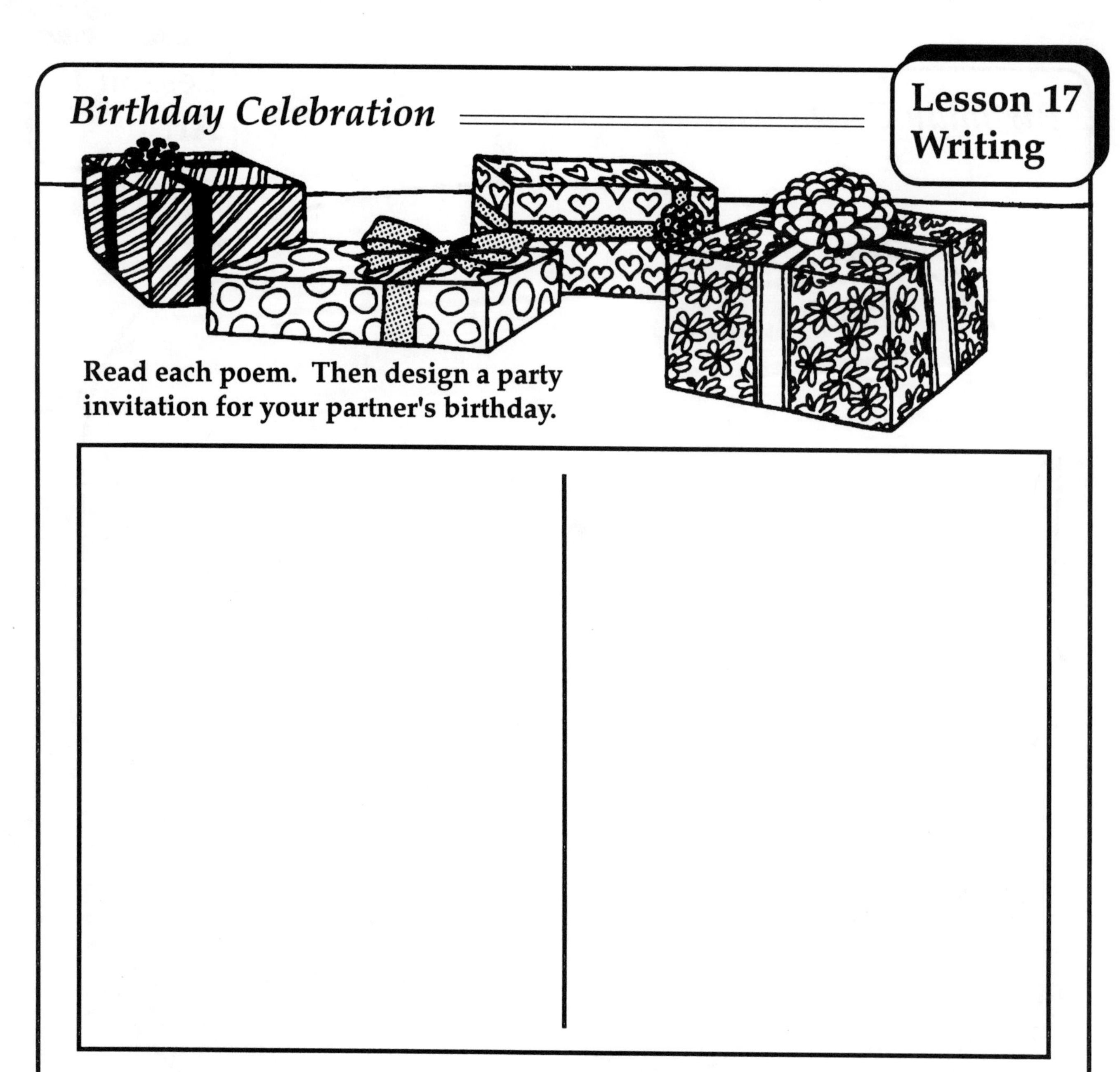

Read each poem. Then design a party invitation for your partner's birthday.

Birthdays
Monday's child is fair of face,
Tuesday's child is full of grace,
Wednesday's child is full of woe,
Thursday's child has far to go,
Friday's child is loving and giving,
Saturday's child has to work for its living
But a child that's born on the Sabbath day
Is fair and wise, and good and gay.

Anonymous

Birthdays
My brother turns out the lights,
It's dark.
We all wait
With excited anticipation
For that special, magic moment,
When mother comes through
The dining room door,
With a big chocolate cake
All aglowing with eleven candles
And one to grow on.

Jane Brucker
La Mesa, California

Lesson 18: Springtime Fun

Overview and Objectives

Many children think of the spring holiday season as a time of special religious significance — a celebration of both Easter and Passover. It would be helpful for the students to share what these holidays mean to them during the pre-lesson discussion period. If you have students from other cultures in the classroom, be sure to encourage them to share any special spring holidays they have and tell how they are celebrated.

Youngsters also think of this season as the time when a big funny rabbit brings candy and when families make brightly-colored eggs, have egg hunts, wear fancy new clothes, and enjoy baskets of goodies.

Lesson 18 is designed to help your students not only share the traditions that accompany spring holidays, but also discuss feelings, both positive and negative, that they associate with this time of the year. This lesson should be a particularly exciting one for your students. At this point of the friendship program, they should be quite comfortable with each other and they'll find the art activity game a great way to have fun together.

Lesson Format

Let the students know that they will be making a gameboard for the Partner Books and playing a game together. Review with the students the interview questions, the instructions for making the gameboard, and the directions for playing the game. It would be helpful to have a gameboard made up ahead of time for the children to see. Remind the partners that even though they will only need one gameboard to play the game , both boards should be made and placed in the Partner Books, so each student will have one.

In the directions for making the gameboard, time is provided for the glue to dry on the spinner wheel. During the drying period, the students can be preparing the spelling cards. Let the class know which spelling words they should use. It might be helpful to create a list of words with the class that have to do with friendship. These should be written on the board.

Since the children do not have to write two sentences at the bottom of the artwork page, allow a little extra time for them to play the game together. The activity will be an excellent way to build a friendship.

The writing page has several poems on it. Ask the partners to read the poems aloud to each other and then write a short story about Easter, Passover, or another spring holiday.

Enrichment and Multicultural Activities

The following activities are designed to promote multicultural awareness, encourage cooperative learning, and incorporate the friendship-building process into an integrated learning curriculum.

These ideas can be used to enhance the lesson for the partners as well as the whole class. All the activities relate to the topic of the lesson.

1. Discuss the Spring holidays May Day or Cinco de Mayo and their meanings.

2. Ask the children to find out the origin of St. Patrick's Day. This will give them a good opportunity to learn about another country and practice their geography skills. The class can research to learn more about the importance of the color green that symbolizes this holiday.

3. Have the class put on a multicultural Spring Parade for the school. Each child can dress in the costume of a different culture.

4. Hold an egg-decorating contest The hunt could be planned by older students for younger children. Award prizes for: funniest, most creative, most unusual, etc.

5. Conduct a class Egg Hunt. Organize the students into groups and let each group be in charge of a various aspect of this project (e.g. planning the hunt, preparing the eggs, deciding who will hide the eggs and who will hunt for them).

6. Have students make shadow boxes showing scenes that represent Easter, Passover, or Spring. Divide students into groups and let each group decide on the theme for a shadow box.

7. Encourage the students to plan a class talent show. The students could present it for the rest of the school as part of a Spring Festival. The students should present their performances in group acts rather

than as individuals.

8. Celebrate spring with a nature walk. Have the partners operate as a team. One child will be the eyes, and another the ears. Each partner will record the signs of Spring that they see or hear. *Use the reproducible sheet on page 168 for this activity.*

9. Let the students plant a flower garden on the school grounds. Have one group of students organize the project and decide what each of the other groups will do.

10. Have a reader's theatre where students share books they have read. The books should have a multicultural theme with peacemaking or acceptance as their focus.

Suggested Children's Literature

The following list of children's books will enhance the focus of this lesson. The use of books with religious themes is left to the discretion of the teacher.

Grades K - 3

- *The Country Bunny* by DuBose Heyward. Houghton Mifflin, 1939.
- *Thirteen Moons on Turtle's Back* by Joseph Bruchac. Philomel, 1991.
- *Easter Fun* by Judith H. Corwin. Little Simon, 1986.
- *Passover Fun: For Little Hands* by Katherine J. Kahn. KarBen, 1991.
- *Easter Parade* by Mary Chalmers. Harper Collins, 1990.
- *Passover Fun Book: Puzzles, Riddles, Magic, & More* by David A. Adler. Hebrew Pub., 1978.
- *Easter & Other Spring Holidays* by Gilda Berger. Watts, 1983.

Grades 4 - 6

- *Book of Holidays Around the World* by Alice van Straalen. Dutton, 1986.
- *The Animal, the Vegetable, and John D. Jones* by Betsy C. Byars. Delacorte, 1982.
- *Summer Business* by Charles E. Martin. Harper & Row, 1990.

Name ______________________________

SPRING IS HERE!

In each column draw pictures or write words that tell about Spring.

THINGS I SEE	THINGS I HEAR	THINGS I DO

Springtime Fun

Lesson 18
Interview

1. Do you celebrate any holidays at this time of year? What are they?

2. Can you tell me the meaning behind the holiday you celebrate?

3. How does your family celebrate this holiday?

4. Have you ever won a prize for collecting the most eggs, or finding the "prize egg" at an egg hunt? How did you feel about that?

5. Have you ever been to a parade? What kind? Do you like parades?

6. What do you do during spring vacation?

7. What does the season of Spring mean to you?

8. What three words describe how you feel about school vacation breaks?

9. What will you do during summer vacation?

10. Will you miss your school friends over the vacation?

11. Did you make any new friends this year in school?

Here are three things we like about springtime.

____

____

____

Springtime Fun

Lesson 18
Art

Materials Needed: markers, crayons, scissors, zip lock sandwich bag, cardboard, glue, brad, 6 index cards, tape, pencil.

Directions:

1. Color the gameboard on the artwork page. Your partner's name goes in the blanks. Tape the sandwich bag on the back of the artwork page for game pieces.

2. Cut out the small boxes on this page to use as markers for the game. Color the animals lightly so you can still see the details.

3. Cut out the wheel and the spinner. Trace the pieces onto cardboard, and cut out. Glue the paper pieces onto the cardboard pieces and let dry.

4. Cut the index cards in half. Write one spelling word on each piece.

5. Carefully punch a hole in the center of the spinner with the tip of your metal brad. Put your brad through the hole and then through the wheel.

6. Read the directions to the game on the artwork page. Play the game with your partner. Have fun!

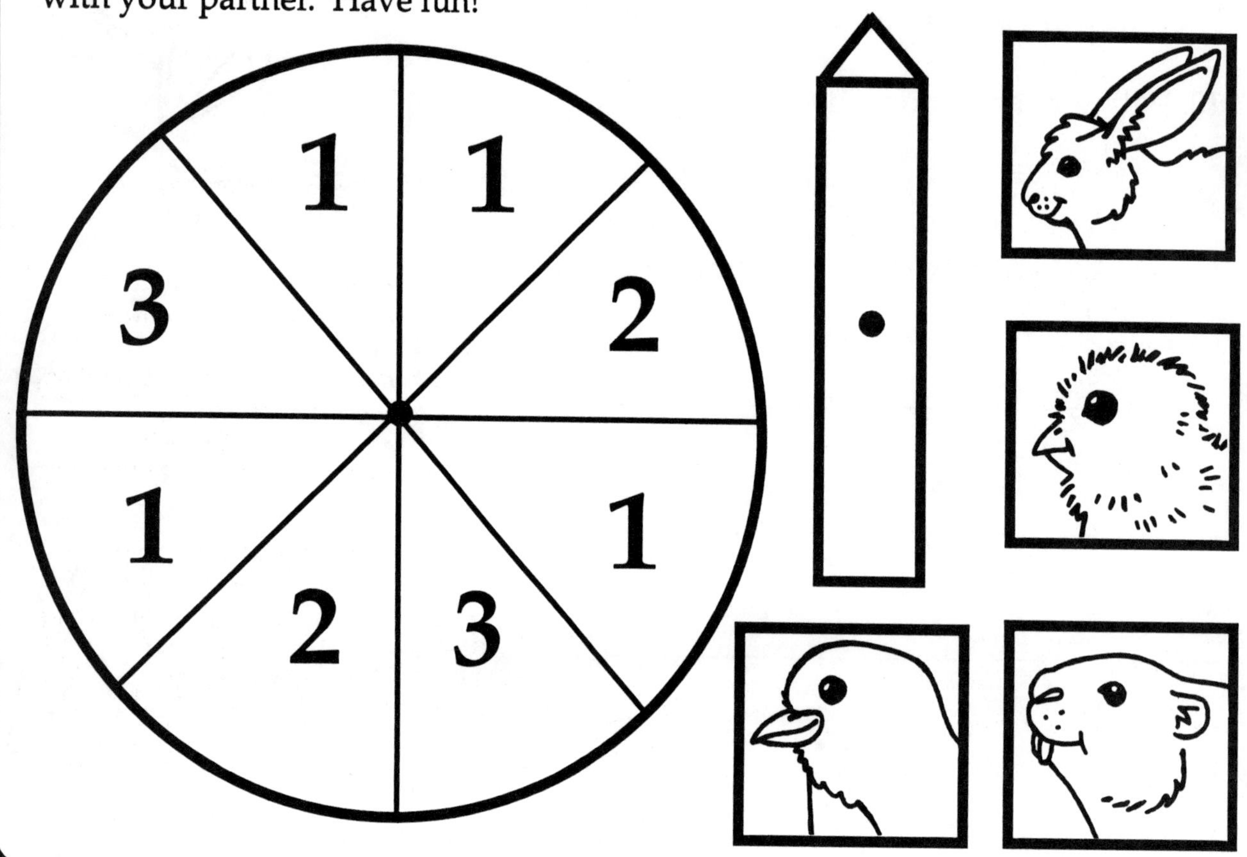

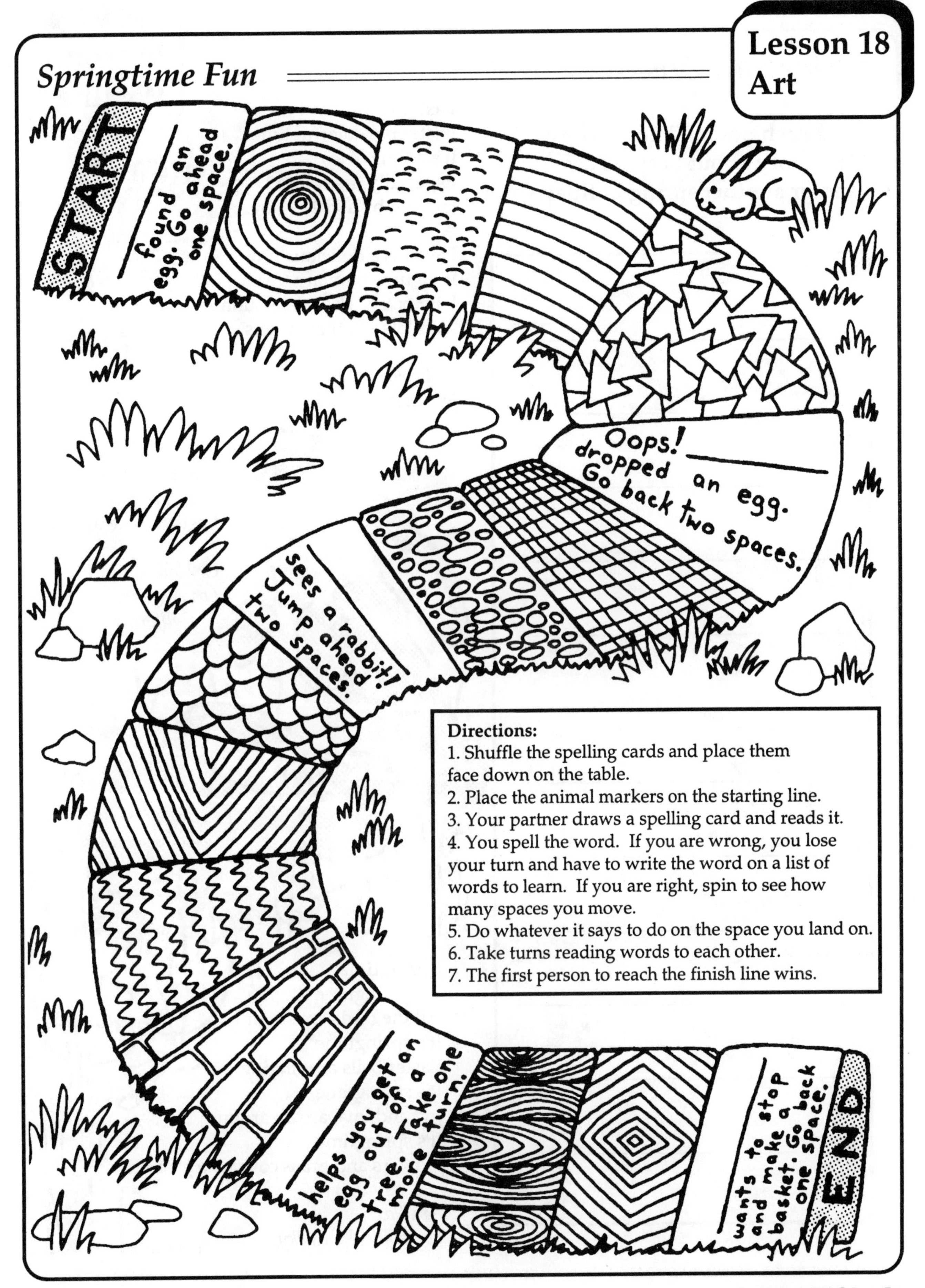
Lesson 18
Art
Springtime Fun
START
found an egg. Go ahead one space.
Oops! dropped an egg. Go back two spaces.
sees a rabbit! Jump ahead two spaces.
helps you get an egg out of a tree. Take one more turn.
wants to stop and make a basket. Go back one space.
END
Directions:
1. Shuffle the spelling cards and place them face down on the table.
2. Place the animal markers on the starting line.
3. Your partner draws a spelling card and reads it.
4. You spell the word. If you are wrong, you lose your turn and have to write the word on a list of words to learn. If you are right, spin to see how many spaces you move.
5. Do whatever it says to do on the space you land on.
6. Take turns reading words to each other.
7. The first person to reach the finish line wins.

Springtime Fun

Lesson 18
Writing

Read each poem. Then write a short story about Easter, Passover, or another spring holiday.

Easter Is
Easter is a colorful time
It's a time of joy,
Especially the colored eggs
Hunted by a girl or boy.

Easter is a delicious time
It's a time of many treats,
Jelly beans, chocolate bunnies
And lots of other sweets.

Leslie Fox
St. Petersburg, Florida

Bunnies hopping
Eggs are popping
Easter's here again!!!

Gordon Settle
Los Angeles, California

Springtime
It's springtime . . .
All the birds are singing
It's springtime . . .
Easter bells are ringing.
It's springtime . . .
Joy and love are all around . . .
It's springtime . . .
Flowers and grass cover the ground.

Ava Fox
Louisville, Kentucky

Partner
Book
To
From

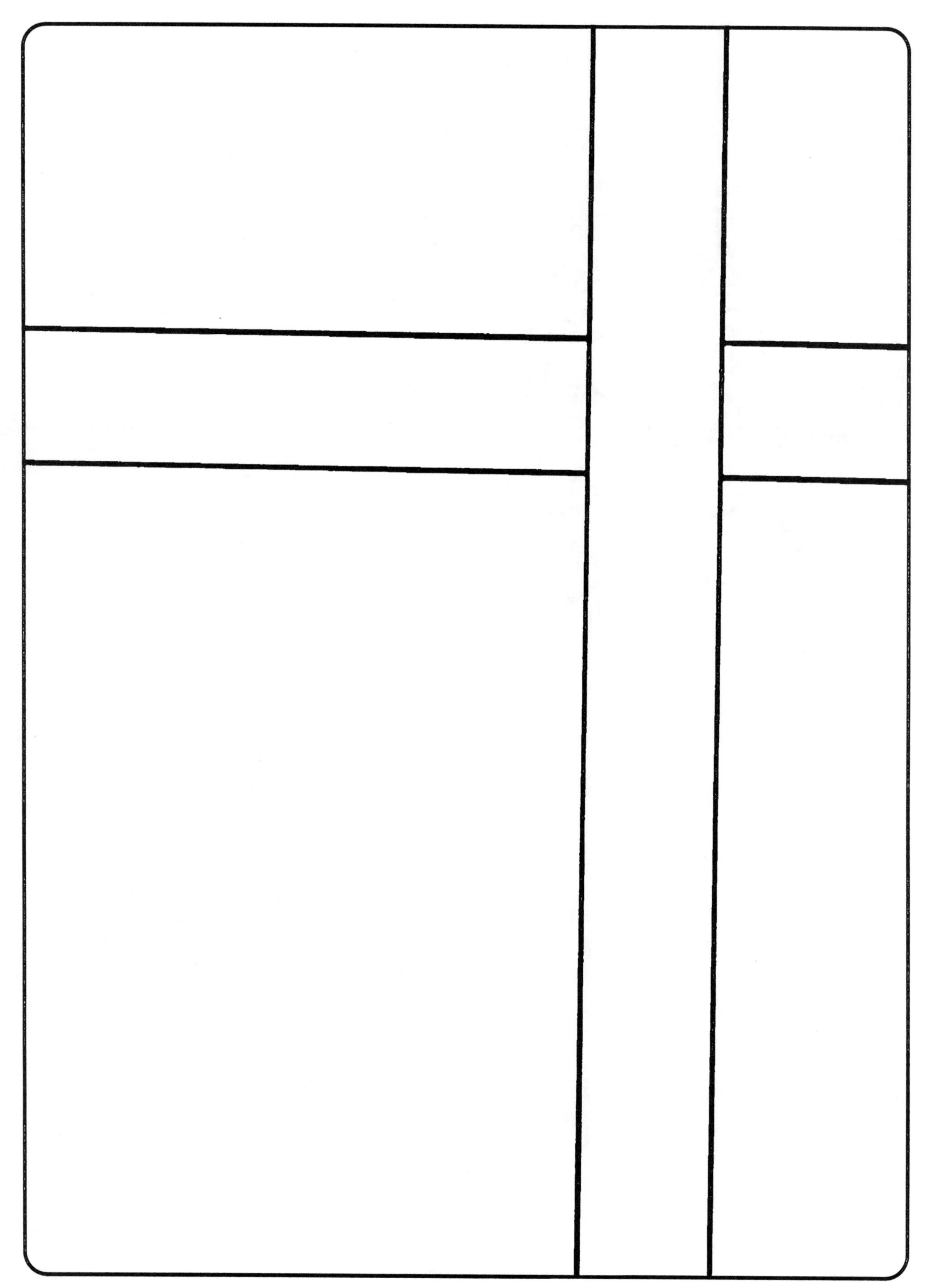

Bibliography

Research Reading
The following books and articles are recommended reading material to help you understand the concept of self-esteem and friendship-building, and their value in the educational field.

Byrne, D. *The Attraction Paradigm.* New York: Academic Press, 1971.

California Task Force to Promote Self-Esteem, *Toward a State of Esteem.* California State Department of Education: Sacramento, CA., 1989.

Cole, J. D., and Dodge, K. A. "Continuities and Change in Children's Social Status: A Five Year Longitudinal Study," *Merrill-Palmer Quarterly,* 1983, *29,* 261-262.

Festinger, L. *A Theory of Cognitive Dissonance.* Stanford, California: Stanford University Press, 1957.

Fox, C. L. "Acceptance of Exceptional Children in the Regular Classroom," *Dissertation Abstracts International,* 1979, *39,* (7), 417a.

Fox, C. L. "Peer Acceptance of Learning Disabled Children in the Regular Classroom," *Exceptional Children,* 1989, *56,* (1), 50-59.

Ladd, G. W. and Mize, J. "A Cognitive Social-Learning Model of Social Skills Training," *Psychological Review,* 1983, *90,* 127-157.

Middleton, H., Zollinger, J. and Keene, R. "Popular Peers as Change Agents for the Socially Neglected Children in the Classroom," *Journal of School Psychology,* 1986, *24* (4), 341-347.

Oden, S. L. and Asher, S. R. *Coaching Children in Social Skills for Friendship-Making,* Paper presented at the Meeting of the society for Research in Child Development, Denver CO.

Rucker, C. N. and Vincenzo, F. M. "Maintaining Social Acceptance Gains Make by EMR Children," *Exceptional Children,* 1970, *36,* 679-680.

Shores, R. E. "Overview of Research on Social Interaction: A Historical and Personal Perspective, *Behavioral Disorders,* 1987, *12,* 233-241.

Walz, Garry and Bleure, Jeanne. *Volume 1 Student Self-Esteem: A Vital Element of School Success.* Ann Arbor, Michigan: Counseling Personnel Services, Inc., 1992.

Wassmer, Arthur C. *Making Contact.* New York: Dial Press, 1978.

Resource Books

The following list is an excellent source for ideas, games, and activities, to incorporate self-esteem into the classroom and to encourage friendship-building skills.

Bedley, Gene. *Climate Creators.* Irvine, CA: People-Wise Publications, 1985.

Borba, Michele. *Esteem Builders.* Rolling Hills Estates, California: Jalmar Press, 1989.

Borba, Michele and Craig. *Self-Esteem, A Classroom Affair.* San Francisco, California: Harper and Row, 1982.

Canfield, Jack and Wells, Harold. *100 Ways to Enhance Self-Concept in the Classroom.* Englewood Cliffs, New Jersey: Prentice-Hall, 1976.

Chase, Larry. *The Other Side of the Report Card: A How-to-Do-It Program for Effective Education.* Glenview, Illinois: Scott, Foresman and Co., 1975.

Crary, Elizabeth. *Kids Can Cooperate,* Seattle: Parenting Press, 1984.

Drew, Naomi. *Learning the Skills of Peacemaking,* Rolling Hills Estates: Jalmar Press, 1989.

Fluegelman, Andrew, ed. *The New Games Book.* Garden City New Jersey: Doubleday, 1976.

Fugitt, Eva. *"He Hit Me Back First!"* Rolling Hills Estates, California: Jalmar Press, 1983.

Goodman, Mary Ellen. *Race Awareness in Young Children.* New York: Collier Books, 1964.

Gordon, Thomas. *Teacher Effectiveness Training.* New York: Peter H. Wyden, 1974.

McDaniel, Sandy and Bielen, Peggy. *Project Self-Esteem,* Rolling Hills Estates: Jalmar Press, 1990.

McGinnis, Jams and Kathleen. *Educating for Peace and Justice.* St. Louis, Missouri: Institute for Peace and Justice, 1981.

Moorman, Chick and Dishon. *Our Classroom: We Can Learn Together.* Englewood Cliffs, Jew Jersey: Prentice-Hall, 1983.

Reasoner, Robert. *Building Self-Esteem: A Comprehensive Program.* Palo Alto, California: Consulting Psychologist Press, 1982.

Reider, Barbara. *A Hooray Kind of Kid: A Child's Self-Esteem and How to Build It.* El Dorado Hills, California: Sierra House, 1988.

Wright, E. *Good Morning Class, I Love You.* Rolling Hills Estates, California: Jalmar Press, 1989.

About the Author

C. Lynn Fox, Ph.D. is an acknowledged expert in the fields of behavior management, self-esteem enhancement, affective education, substance abuse, and parent training. She has given hundreds of workshops throughout the country and has presented at educational conferences reaching over 100,000 teachers, administrators, parents, and other helping professionals.

The author serves on the advisory board of the National Council for Self-Esteem and the California State Panel to Promote Self-Esteem and Personal and Social Responsibility. She has written nearly a dozen books and training manuals as well as numerous articles on some of the most crucial concerns among educators and community leaders today: communication, self-concept enhancement, and the creation of drug-free schools and communities.

Currently a Professor of Secondary/Post-secondary Education at San Francisco State University, Dr. Fox is also a consultant for national, state, and local educational agencies and school districts. Named Woman of the Year by the California Commission of Alcohol and Drug Dependencies, Dr. Fox has been awarded two major U.S. Department of Education grants to develop comprehensive models to fight drug abuse in schools and to train parents.

Dr. Fox is available to give workshops and consult. Please contact her at:
San Francisco State University
Dept. of Secondary Education
Attn: Lynn Fox, Ph.D.
1600 Holloway
San Francisco, California 94132
(415) 338-2265

Things I've Tried That Worked

Please share your activites with us!

Name: ______________________ Phone: (   ) ______________________

Position ______________________ School ______________________

Address: ______________________ City/State/Zip ______________________

Activites:

1. ____
____
____
____

2. ____
____
____
____

3. ____
____
____
____

4. ____
____
____
____

5. ____
____
____
____

Please mail to: **C. Lynn Fox, Ph. D.**
Professor of Education
Department of Secondary/Postsecondary Education
San Francisco State University
1600 Holloway Avenue
San Francisco, California 94132

Or Fax to: (415) 435-3992

Order NOW 10% Discount On 3 Or More Titles!

20+ YEARS AWARD WINNING PUBLISHER JP

DISCOVER books on self-esteem for kids.

ENJOY great reading with Warm Fuzzies and Squib, the adventurous owl.

Larry Shles, M.A.

Moths & Mothers/Feathers & Fathers: The Story of Squib, The Owl, Begins (Ages 5-105)

Heartwarming story of a tiny owl who cannot fly or hoot as he learns to put words with his feelings. He faces frustration, grief, fear, guilt and loneliness in his life, just as we do. Struggling with these *feelings*, he searches, at least, for *understanding*. *Delightfully illustrated*. Ageless.

0-915190-57-5, 72 pages, **JP-9057-5 $7.95**
8½ x 11, paperback, illustrations

Hoots & Toots & Hairy Brutes: The Continuing Adventures of Squib, The Owl (Ages 5-105)

Squib, who can only toot, sets out to learn how to give a mighty hoot. Even the *owl-odontist* can't help and he fails completely. Every reader who has struggled with *life's limitations* will recognize his own *struggles* and *triumphs* in the microcosm of Squib's forest world. A parable for all ages.

0-915190-56-7, 72 pages, **JP-9056-7 $7.95**
8½ x 11, paperback, illustrations

Larry Shles, M.A.

NOT JUST AUTHORS BUT RESEARCHERS AND PRACTITIONERS.

Larry Shles, M.A.

Hugs & Shrugs: The Continuing Saga of Squib, The Owl (Ages 5-105)

Squib feels *lonely*, *depressed* and *incomplete*. His reflection in the pond shows that he has lost a piece of himself. He thinks his missing piece fell out and he searches in vain outside of himself to find it. Only when he discovers that it fell in and not out does he *find inner-peace* and *become whole*. Delightfully illustrated. Ageless.

0-915190-47-8, 72 pages, **JP-9047-8 $7.95**
8½ x 11, paperback, illustrations

Aliens in my Nest: Squib Meets the Teen Creature (Ages 5-105)

What does it feel like to face a snarly, surly, defiant and non-communicative older brother turned *adolescent*? Friends, dress code, temperament, entertainment, room decor, eating habits, authority, music, isolation, *internal and external conflict* and many other *areas of change* are *dealt with*. Explores how to handle every situation.

0-915190-49-4, 80 pages, **JP-9049-4 $7.95**
8½ x 11, paperback, illustrations

Larry Shles, M.A.

NOT JUST WRITTEN BUT PROVEN EFFECTIVE.

Larry Shles, M.A.

Do I Have to Go to School Today? Squib Measures Up! (Ages 5-105)

Squib *dreads* going to *school*. He day-dreams about all the reasons he has not to go: the school bus will swallow him, the older kids will be mean to him, numbers and letters confuse him, he is too small for sports, etc. But, in the end, he *goes because* his *teacher accepts him "just as he is."* Very esteeming. Great metaphor for all ages.

0-915190-62-1, 64 pages, **JP-9062-1 $7.95**
8½ x 11, paperback, illustrations

Scooter's Tail of Terror A Fable of Addiction and Hope (Ages 5-105)

Well-known author and illustrator, Larry Shles, introduces a new forest character — a squirrel named Scooter. He faces the challenge of addiction, but is offered a way to overcome it. As with the Squib books, the story is *simple*, yet the message is *dramatic*. The story touches the child within each reader and *presents the realities of addiction*.

0-915190-89-3, 80 pages, **JP-9089-3 $9.95**
8½x 11, paperback, illustrations

NEW

Larry Shles, M.A.

100% TESTED — 100% PRACTICAL — 100% GUARANTEED.

REVISED

Alvyn Freed, Ph.D.

TA for Tots (and other prinzes) Revised (Gr. PreK-3)

Over 500,000 sold. New upright format. Book has helped thousands of young *children* and their *parents* to better *understand* and *relate to each other*. Helps youngsters realize their *intrinsic worth* as human beings; builds and strengthens their *self-esteem*. *Simple* to understand.
Coloring Book $1.95 / I'm OK Poster $3

0-915190-73-7, 144 pages, **JP-9073-7 $14.95**
8½ x 11, paperback, delightful illustrations

TA for Kids (and grown-ups too) (Gr. 4-9)

Over 250,000 sold. An ideal book to help youngsters *develop self-esteem*, esteem of others, *personal and social responsibility*, critical thinking and independent judgment. Book recognizes that each person is a unique human being with the capacity to learn, grow and develop. Hurray for TA! Great for parents and other care givers.

0-915190-09-5, 112 pages, **JP-9009-5 $9.95**
8½ x 11, paperback, illustrations

Alvyn Freed, Ph.D. & Margaret Freed

ORDER NOW FOR 10% DISCOUNT ON 3 OR MORE TITLES.

Alvyn Freed, Ph.D.

TA for Teens (and other important people) (Gr. 8-12)

Over 100,000 sold. The book that tells teenagers they're OK! Provides help in growing into adulthood in a mixed-up world. Contrasts freedom and irresponsibility with knowing that *youth need* the *skill, determination* and *inner strength* to reach *fulfillment* and *self-esteem*. No talking down to kids, here.

0-915190-03-6, 258 pages, **JP-9003-6 $21.95**
8½ x 11, paperback, illustrations

The Original Warm Fuzzy Tale (Gr. Pre K-Adult)

Over 100,000 sold. The concept of Warm Fuzzies and Cold Pricklies originated in this delightful story. A *fairy tale* in every sense, *with* adventure, fantasy, heroes, villians and a *moral*. Children (and adults, too) will enjoy this beautifully illustrated book. **Songs of Warm Fuzzy Cass. $12.95. Warm Fuzzies, JP-9042 $0.99 each.**

0-915190-08-7, 48 pages, **JP-9008-7 $8.95**
6 x 9, paperback, full color illustrations

Claude Steiner, Ph.D

ORDER FROM: B.L. Winch & Associates/Jalmar Press, Skypark Business Center, 2675 Skypark Drive, Suite 204 , Torrance, CA 90505
CALL TOLL FREE — (800) 662-9662 • (310) 784-0016 • FAX (310) 784-1379 • Add 10% shipping; $3 minimum

5/93

Order NOW 10% Discount On 3 Or More Titles!

OPEN your mind to wholebrain thinking and creative parenting.

GROW by leaps and bounds with our new ways to think and learn.

Openmind/Wholemind: Parenting and Teaching Tomorrow's Children Today (Staff/Personal)

Can we learn to *treat* the *brain/mind system* as *open* rather than closed? Can we learn to *use all* our *learning modalities, learning styles, creativities* and *intelligences* to create a product far greater than the sum of its parts? Yes! This primer for parents and teachers shows how.

Bob Samples, M.A.

0-915190-45-1, 272 pages, **JP-9045-1 $14.95**
7 x 10, paperback, 81 B/W photos, illust.

Unicorns Are Real: A Right-Brained Approach to Learning (Gr. K-Adult)

Over 100,000 sold. The *alternate methods* of *teaching/learning* developed by the author have helped literally thousands of children and adults with *learning difficulties*. A book of *simple ideas* and *activities* that are easy to use, yet dramatically effective. Video of techniques also available: **VHS, 1½ hrs., JP-9113-0 $149.95. Unicorn Poster $4.95.**

0-915190-35-4, 144 pages, **JP-9035-4 $12.95**
8½ x 11, paperback, illus., assessment

Barbara Meister Vitale, M.A.

NOT JUST AUTHORS BUT RESEARCHERS AND PRACTITIONERS.

REVISED

Metaphoric Mind: A Celebration of Creative Consciousness (Revised) (Staff/Personal)

A plea for a balanced way of thinking and being in a culture that stands on the knife-edge between *catastrophe* and *transformation*. The metaphoric mind is *asking* again, quietly but insistently, *for equilibrium*. For, after all, equilibrium is the way of nature. A revised version of a classic.

Bob Samples, M.A.

0-915190-68-0, 272 pages, **JP-9068-0 $16.95**
7 x 10, paperback, B/W photos, illus.

Free Flight: Celebrating Your Right Brain (Staff/Personal)

Journey with Barbara Meister Vitale, from her uncertain childhood perceptions of being *"different"* to the acceptance and adult celebration of that difference. A how to *book for right-brained people* in a *left-brained world*. Foreword by Bob Samples- *"This book is born of the human soul."* Great gift item for your right-brained friends.

0-915190-44-3, 128 pages, **JP-9044-3 $9.95**
5½ x 8½, paperback, illustrations

Barbara Meister Vitale, M.A.

NOT JUST WRITTEN BUT PROVEN EFFECTIVE.

NEW

Imagine That! Getting Smarter Through Imagery Practice (Gr. K-Adult)

Understand and *develop* your own *seven intelligences* in only minutes a day. Help children do the same. The results will amaze you. Clear, step-by-step ways show you how to create your own imagery exercises for any area of learning or life and how to *relate imagery* exercises *to curriculum content*.

Lane Longino Waas, Ph.D.

0-915190-71-0, 144 pages, **JP-9071-0 $12.95**
6 x 9, paperback, 42 B/W photos, biblio.

NEW

Becoming Whole (Learning) Through Games (Gr. K-Adult)

New ideas for old games. *Develop* your *child's brain power, motivation* and *self-esteem by playing*. An excellent parent/ teacher guide and skills checklist to 100 standard games. Included are auditory, visual, motor, directional, modality, attention, educational, social and memory skills. Great resource for care givers.

0-915190-70-2, 288 pages, **JP-9070-2 $16.95**
6 x 9, paperback, glossary, biblio.

Gwen Bailey Moore, Ph.D. & Todd Serby

100% TESTED — 100% PRACTICAL — 100% GUARANTEED.

Present Yourself: Great Presentation Skills (Staff/Personal)

Use *mind mapping* to become a presenter who is a dynamic part of the message. Learn about transforming fear, knowing your audience, setting the stage, making them remember and much more. *Essential reading* for anyone interested in *communication*. This book will become the standard work in its field. **Hardback, JP-9050-8 $16.95**

Michael J. Gelb, M.A.

0-915190-51-6, 128 pages, **JP-9051-6 $9.95**
6 x 9, paperback, illus., mind maps

The Two Minute Lover (Staff/Personal)

With wit, wisdom and compassion, "The Two-Minute Lovers" and their proteges guide you through the steps of *building* and *maintaining* an *effective relationship in a fast-paced world*. They offer encouragement, inspiration and practical techniques for living happily in a relationship, even when outside pressures are enormous. Done like the "One Minute Manager".

0-915190-52-4, 112 pages, **JP-9052-4 $9.95**
6 x 9, paperback, illustrations

Asa Sparks, Ph.D.

ORDER NOW FOR 10% DISCOUNT ON 3 OR MORE TITLES.

The Turbulent Teens: Understanding Helping, Surviving (Parents/Counselors)

Come to grips with the difficult issues of rules and the limits of parental tolerance, recognizing the necessity for *flexibility* that takes into consideration changes in the adolescent as well as the imperative *need for control*, agreed upon *expectations* and *accountability*. A must read! Useful in counseling situations.

James E. Gardner, Ph.D.

0-913091-01-4, 224 pages, **JP-9101-4 $8.95**
6 x 9, paperback, case histories

The Parent Book: Raising Emotionally Mature Children - Ages 3-15 (Parents)

Improve *positive bonding* with your child in five easy steps: *listen* to the feelings; *learn* the basic concern; *develop* an action plan; *confront* with support; *spend* 1 to 1 time. Ideas for helping in 4 *self-esteem* related areas: *awareness; relating; competence; integrity*. 69 sub-catagories. Learn what's missing and what to do about it.

0-915190-15-X, 208 pages, **JP-9015-X $9.95**
8½ x 11, paperback, illus., diag/Rx.

Howard Besell, Ph.D. & Thomas P. Kelly, Jr.

ORDER FROM: B.L. Winch & Associates/Jalmar Press, Skypark Business Center, 2675 Skypark Drive, Suite 204, Torrance, CA 90505
CALL TOLL FREE — (800) 662-9662 • (310) 784-0016 • FAX (310) 784-1379 • Add 10% shipping; $3 minimum

5/93